# Stay With Me, Rhys

## The heartbreaking story of Rhys Jones

### MELANIE JONES

3 5 7 9 10 8 6 4 2

Virgin Books, an imprint of Ebury Publishing,
20 Vauxhall Bridge Road,
London SW1V 2SA

Virgin Books is part of the Penguin Random House group of
companies whose addresses can be found at
global.penguinrandomhouse.com

Penguin
Random House
UK

First published in the United Kingdom by Virgin Books in 2018

www.penguin.co.uk

A CIP catalogue record for this book is available from the
British Library

ISBN 9780753552292

Typeset in 11.5/18.5 pt ITC Giovanni Std
by Integra Software Services Pvt. Ltd, Pondicherry

Printed and bound in Great Britain by Clays Ltd, St Ives PLC

Penguin Random House is committed to a sustainable future for our
business, our readers and our planet. This book is made from
Forest Stewardship Council® certified paper.

*To Owen, who gave me a reason to get up every morning
and the strength to carry on*

## A Mother Holds Her Baby
**by Stephen Jones**

Quietly she holds him, cradled in her arms
Rocking oh so gently, protecting him from harm
Her tears are flowing freely, off her cheeks they race
Always heading downwards, then dripping from her face
A mother holds her baby, as close as close can be
And as his eyes stare skyward, there's only her to see
Now fast forward eleven years, the scene is much the same
A mother holds her baby, whispering his name
Ruffling his matted hair, his face covered in blood
Telling him to stay with her and wrapping him in love
But the child will never answer, forever to stay young
Dying on a car park, it's not where he belongs
A mother holds her baby, her child, her world, her son
His life has been robbed from him, she can't believe he's gone
One last hug, one last caress to his cheek – a simple kiss
To thank that little boy for eleven years of bliss

# CONTENTS

# PROLOGUE

My husband Ste called me out into the front garden where he was lopping bits off a big leylandii. If left to its own devices, the tree went a bit wild, so it needed regular topping and trimming, and that weekend he had decided it needed cutting back.

'Mel,' he called. 'Come outside a minute.'

I opened the front door and stepped out and he said, 'Look what I just found.'

There, halfway up the trunk of the tree, was a carving that read 'RJ-07', which must have been chipped into the bark by my wonderful, cheeky, lovable son Rhys Jones two years before.

'I never knew he'd done that,' said Ste.

Tears started in my eyes, as they so often did, but at the same time it made me smile. Rhys would have carved those initials just weeks, or days, before he was taken away from us, the victim of a senseless crime. In August of that same year, as he walked home from football practice, he was hit by a stray bullet fired by a callous teenager caught up in a gangland feud, and he died on the trauma table just two hours later. Our world had been shattered in a split second and our lives would never be complete again.

Now Rhys's initials, carved into the wood, stood as a constant reminder that he had been there, a normal, mischievous eleven-year-old, making his mark on the world just like he left his mark on my heart. A mark that would never fade.

# CHAPTER ONE

# Our Boy Blue

**ON A COLD** Sunday afternoon in October 2006, I stood at the side of a football pitch with my husband Ste, huddled up in my thickest winter coat, watching our boy Rhys playing for the local team. It was the same routine every weekend since he'd signed up to play for Fir Tree Football Club, and we never missed a game, but this one turned out to be special.

It was a hard-fought match and the Fir Tree boys were drawing 0–0 when they won a free kick from twenty yards. Rhys stepped up to take it. He ran up to the ball and, with his left foot, which was always the strongest, he skilfully curled it over the wall and into the net. GOAL! It was absolutely fabulous. Ste and I were jumping up and down with excitement. Rhys was running around the pitch in his own jubilant goal celebration and, suddenly, he lifted his shirt to reveal a T-shirt underneath that read, 'This one is for the troops.' We had no idea what that was all about and it remains a mystery to this day, as Rhys never really explained it. He was always full of surprises and the reason was lost in the moment as he was mobbed by his fellow players, ecstatic at the spectacular finish to the game. He went on to win Goal of the Season for that stunning display of skill. The trophy he was awarded became his most treasured possession, taking pride of place in his bedroom, among numerous other trophies he had won from his favourite sport.

Rhys was a natural on the football pitch. One of my earliest memories of him is kicking a ball around the living room at nine months, still in his baby walker. By the time he was two, he would spend hours with Ste and his older brother Owen having a kickabout in the garden and when Rhys was five, Ste would take the boys to the park on a Sunday for a game of football. He would give the boys 50p each for every goal they scored and if Ste saved the goal they would give him 10p. Ste always came home skint!

While he was always running around as a lad, Rhys was in no hurry to make his first appearance. He was born on 27 September 1995, three days overdue, and it was a long and traumatic labour.

My waters broke in the early hours of the morning, and I leapt out of bed just in time. I remember thinking, 'Thank goodness I got out of bed, or I would have had to buy a new mattress.'

Ste was asleep, so I woke him up and told him I was in labour. Owen, our older son, was five at the time so we got him out of bed and bundled him in the car, then we dropped him at my sister Debra's, and made our way to the labour ward at the hospital in Fazakerley, just a five-minute drive from our home in Liverpool.

My labour pains were not helped by one particular nurse who seemed to be in much more of a hurry than Rhys was. She kept looking at her watch and saying, 'Come on Mrs Jones. I finish at half past two. Get a move on.' I was giving Ste a look that, after ten years of marriage, he was easily able to interpret as a sign I was about to explode. Ste was talking to me in a soothing voice and trying to keep me calm, but she just kept on saying, 'Come on Mrs Jones.' Honest to God, I could have given her a slap! Childbirth is stressful enough without her putting the pressure on.

Apparently I wasn't the only one feeling the strain. When another nurse put a monitor on my stomach, to hear the heartbeat, she said, 'This baby is getting stressed,' and Little Miss Impatience immediately declared, 'Right. She's going to have a Caesar.' Presumably, that would have meant she could knock off on time.

Eventually, her colleague decided to fetch a doctor and he calmed the situation down, saying the baby would come when he was ready. As soon as everything was calm, Rhys was born naturally, weighing in at a healthy 7lb 12oz. It was 2.25 precisely – so the nurse was all right. She got to clock off on time after all.

Rhys's birth was the complete opposite to our first son Owen, born in March 1990. Owen was a textbook birth. He was born on the due date: my waters broke, I went into labour and an hour and a half later Owen appeared. It was all fine, no stress and at the time I thought, 'If this is what it's about, I'll have six!' But with Rhys's birth, the nurse had me so agitated with her 'Come on Mrs Jones,' I was fuming. After that I said, 'That's it. I'm not having any more.'

To add insult to injury, I was thirty when I had Rhys and I will always remember that the hospital wrote on my notes 'Geriatric mother.' That made me feel terrible. How dare I have a baby at thirty! Nowadays everyone has them after thirty but it wasn't so common then. Admittedly I was the oldest woman on my ward, but I couldn't believe that they put 'geriatric' on my notes. It made me feel about eighty.

We named our bouncing baby boy Rhys Milford Jones, choosing the middle name as a tribute to my dad, Milford Edwards. At the time of Rhys's birth, my dad had already been diagnosed with a terminal brain tumour and only had a short while left. Although he only knew Rhys for four and a half months, he was so very proud of both the boys and loved them to bits.

Rhys was a happy baby. He fed well and ate well until he was a toddler. Then suddenly, at about the age of eighteen months, he started to have a real problem with food. He would go for days and not eat, or at least it felt like days to me. Every time we sat down to have a meal, there were issues. It wasn't something I had come across before because Owen would eat anything you put in front of him but Rhys was a really picky eater. He must have eaten along the way but I was really worried he wasn't getting enough nutrition so, in the end, I took him to the doctor and told him we were having issues with food. The doctor weighed him and measured him and said he was just average for his age.

'Some days he doesn't want to eat and other days he doesn't stop,' I said. But the doctor assured me there was nothing to worry about.

'What he's doing is fine,' he said. 'Let him eat what he wants to eat. You're getting more stressed than he is,' which was true. His advice was simple.

'Put the food in front of him and if he doesn't eat it, that's fine,' he said. 'Just don't give him anything else.' That's exactly what we did and, within three or four months, he was eating normally.

Owen was really happy when Rhys was born and he was really good with him. We'd told him he was getting a baby brother or sister, but in those days you didn't find out what you were having beforehand so he was dead chuffed when he found out it was a boy.

Rhys was a joker, always laughing, always wanting to play tricks. He never stopped messing about, but in a good way, never in a malicious way. Although they always got on brilliantly, he and Owen were like chalk and cheese. Owen was quiet and shy, and found it hard to approach people he didn't know. He would wait for them to come and talk to him. But Rhys was incredibly outgoing. If we were on holiday and he saw other kids playing, he'd say, 'I'm just going to go and play with them,' and he'd be off. He would think nothing of approaching them and would be part of their game within seconds. He just got on with everyone.

The house where we lived was on a quiet residential estate near Croxteth Country Park, a 500-acre plot of woodland and greenery that surrounds Croxteth Hall.

Rhys was very happy growing up on our estate, and he made plenty of friends. The kids in the street always used to knock on the door and ask for him to come out and play with them, and he didn't need asking twice. He was usually the first person they knocked for because they knew, if Rhys was out, there would soon be enough of their friends for a game of footie or hide and seek.

If he wasn't out somewhere with them, they would be kicking a ball around at ours. We had two goalie nets that we put up in the garden and we even swapped the grass for AstroTurf because, even though our garden is tiny, we had every kid in the street playing football whenever they got the chance. Sometimes, usually when I was out and Ste was in charge, they'd put the two wheelie bins by the garage and use those as a goal. Our garage still has big dents in the metal door but Ste won't knock them out because he says, 'That's what Rhys did.'

When Rhys was little, Owen used to love having a bit of a kickabout with him in the garden but, as he got towards the end of primary school, he had a lot of problems with his knees and he had to go for treatment at Alder Hey Children's Hospital. He had

had a massive growth spurt and the specialist said he had a common knee problem called Osgood–Schlatter disease, meaning his bones were growing too quickly for his muscles, which were being overstretched.

'You have two options,' the doctor said. 'You either stop playing sport altogether and let the bones and ligaments catch up with each other. Or you carry on and both your legs will be in plaster for six months.' Owen chose to stop playing sport and became an armchair football pundit instead.

Rhys would never have had that growth spurt, I don't think, and he wasn't destined to be as tall as Owen. They were different from day one. Owen was 6lb 10oz at birth but he was always quite stocky, and took after his dad, while Rhys was small and slight and took after me a bit more.

While Owen couldn't play football for a team, he would still have a kickabout with his little brother in the garden or the park and they still bonded over their passion for the beautiful game. The whole house is a football house and Everton was an obsession for both the boys.

Ste and I took Rhys to his first Everton match at Goodison Park, along with Owen, when he was about three. We all used to go as a family treat as often as we could and Rhys was very excited at the first match. The pitch at Goodison Park is curved, and if you are in the family section you can't see the white line on the other side and you don't know if the ball has gone out. That used to frustrate him because he couldn't see where the ball was, and we had to look at the screen to see if it was out of play. It drove him mad and he used to stand on the seat because he couldn't see. The first few times we went he didn't like the loud noises that the crowd made but nothing would have stopped him going back. He was already hooked.

Rhys was a Blue through and through. He looked forward to his Saturday afternoons at the footie every week, and he'd start getting excited about three weeks before the start of the season. But half the time, by October all three of them had lost heart. With every bad match, Rhys would get a real cob on. He would come home and say, 'They should have brought him on!' and 'What did they do that for?' But what always made me howl with laughter was that they would go to the game and then come home grumbling about how bad it was and then watch it all again, if I'd recorded it, or watch *Match of the Day*.

I never understood that. Why put yourselves through it all over again?

Then again, he was always jubilant when the Blues were winning. On one occasion, when Rhys was eight, the three boys had been to the match and watched Everton beat West Ham, 1–0. They were all pretty elated as they piled into the car to make their way home. As usual, Owen was in the front and Rhys was in the back and, when Ste pulled up next to a West Ham coach full of supporters, Rhys couldn't resist getting a dig in. He put his hands up to the window, making the one and the nil signs with his fingers, to rub their faces in it. That was Rhys to a tee. He loved a bit of football banter.

The Saturday routine for the three boys was always the same. Ste would park up by Cherry Lane and walk past Walton Lane Police Station, up towards Goodison Park. Before they went in there was a chippy where they would stop and buy something to eat. They always had curry and rice and a sausage because, Ste said, the chips were awful! Then they would stand around outside while they ate before walking to the ground.

Because Ste liked to leave plenty of time, they always got there really, really early. Ste always bought two programmes and the boys would both read them from front to back while the players came out and did their warm-up.

Their seats were on the top balcony, which was less rowdy than other parts of the stadium and I was pleased about that. Ste didn't enrol in the autocup scheme, which meant that you were likely to get your usual seats for the FA Cup or League Cup matches, so occasionally they had to sit somewhere else. At one cup match they sat in the park end and two little lads were sitting in front of them. Rhys was nine or ten and Ste said they couldn't have been much older, maybe eleven, but the language out of them was absolutely awful – effing and jeffing all over the place. It was too much for young kids. You don't want them to be hearing that. I was just glad that they usually sat in the family enclosure or the top balcony.

Ste and the boys always hung on until the end and never left early, even if Everton were getting stuffed.

Even today, Ste and Owen follow roughly the same routine, although they time it better so they don't get there so early, and the curry and rice is now a beer and a pie at the stadium. Owen still reads the programme from front to back before the match starts.

Rhys took his love of the team very seriously. Every new kit that came out he'd want to go and buy it and, when he got it, he'd wear it until it fell off him. His bedroom was decorated in Everton colours, his duvet set was Everton and his walls were plastered with posters of the players. Up until 2004, Rhys had a poster of Wayne Rooney on his bedroom wall. Rooney had grown up in Croxteth and ended up playing for Everton so, to Rhys, he was a real role model. He dreamed of following in his footsteps and his football coaches had often remarked that he may well have the talent to go far. But when Rooney announced he was leaving Everton to move to Manchester United, Rhys felt his hero had betrayed the team. He was so upset he poked the eyes out of the poster.

Rhys would eat, sleep and breathe football. If he wasn't playing it outside in the garden, or going to the match, he was playing a football game on Owen's Xbox. Outside of school, football was his life. He had an all-consuming passion for it. Occasionally he would watch wrestling and play with wrestling figures, and he was obsessed with the *Star Wars* films, collecting loads of the little figures of Darth Vader, Luke Skywalker and Yoda, which he would play with a lot, but football came before everything else. If it was a choice between anything else and football, football would win.

At the age of seven, Rhys started playing for the local team, Witty's. In 2005, his third season with the first team, he was playing in a cup game that went to penalties. Rhys was last to take a penalty and the whole match hung on him hitting the back of the net for a win. By the time he lined up, the games on the surrounding pitches had all finished, and players and spectators had all gravitated towards the Witty's match, so there was quite a crowd. Rhys took the penalty and scored – only to have the goal disallowed because the referee said he had kicked the ball before he had blown the whistle. But, to Rhys's delight, he allowed him to retake the penalty and we all stood with bated breath on the sidelines, hearts in our mouths, willing him to score again.

Rhys ran up to the ball, struck it hard and it soared past the goalie and into the net. What a celebration! The jubilant team jumped on Rhys and we were all screaming at the side. It was a great day.

Despite his successes at Witty's, Rhys didn't really get on with the manager. Even at that young age, he thought he knew more about football than anybody else and he just wanted to get on the pitch and play. After three seasons there with them he went to play for Fir Tree FC, who played close to our house, and he loved it there. Because he was that little bit older, and craving a bit of independence, he wanted to walk there and back on his own and, because the pitch where they played and trained was close to home, we let him. He would sometimes walk on his own and other times he would meet his mates on the corner and they'd walk up together. They'd all grown up with each other and they used to go to training once a week and play football together in between.

He loved playing for Fir Tree, and the coach Steve Geoghegan, who was also the father of Rhys's friend Sean, loved Rhys too. Although Rhys was always messing about and starting mud fights, Steve said he was a 'cracking player' and soon guaranteed him a place in every match. While most of the boys had to take their turn on the bench, Steve told us that he wanted Rhys to start on the pitch in every game because he thought he was a really talented player. 'He could sign for any team, I reckon,' he said.

Rhys really threw his all into the team and he never missed a training session no matter what the weather.

Ste and I would go and watch the matches every weekend, rain or shine. In the 2006–2007 season, one game stands out in my mind. I had told Rhys that I would give him £5 if he scored in the match but, with five minutes to go, Fir Tree FC were losing the game, 2–1. Suddenly Rhys booted the ball into the back of the net, levelling the score, and, bubbling with excitement, he ran over to me at the side of the pitch and jumped up into my arms. It was a lovely moment.

Mind you, Rhys didn't take losing well. On one occasion, Fir Tree were playing in the Colts Cup final and they lost. Rhys was so unhappy about receiving the runners-up trophy that he refused to smile for the team photos.

Rhys was always keen on school. Just before his fifth birthday, in 2000, he would follow his big brother into Broad Square primary and he was really great about going into school for the first day, probably because he'd already been in nursery, so he was used to being around lots of kids, and Owen was already in the school. I think it's easier for a second child to go into school, if Rhys is anything to go by. They're used to playing with other children, because they have an older sibling, and in Rhys's case, he had loved nursery and made lots of friends there, so he was pleased to be moving up with them.

Rhys and Owen both loved school. They never wanted to be off, even when they really were sick, and I had no problems getting them up and getting them off to school. They just wanted to be with their mates and saw it as a social thing.

After a while, Rhys began asking to go to breakfast club at school in the morning. Initially, I said no – mainly because I didn't want to get up and get ready any earlier than I already did on a normal school morning – but he kept on.

'You can have your breakfast here. I make you breakfast every morning,' I told him. That wasn't good enough.

'But I want to go to breakfast club, Mum, because then we have time to play football,' he would say. Naturally, football had to be behind the enthusiasm to get to school early.

Eventually, when he was about seven, I relented and he started to go to breakfast club every morning. Thankfully, the teachers did insist he ate *something* there and told him, 'You can't go out to play until you've eaten some breakfast,' otherwise he probably wouldn't have bothered. It was purely for the football, not the breakfast, but they wouldn't let him have breakfast at home and then play, so I ended up dragging myself out of bed earlier to take him every morning.

In 2005, when Rhys was nine and Owen was fourteen, we were due to go on a family holiday to the Greek island of Kos and the kids were really excited. I like to be prepared, so I always get the cases down from the loft two weeks before we go and start putting things into them. I had already started packing when I got a phone call from the travel agent, saying they had double-booked us and they had to cancel the holiday.

After the initial shock, my first thought was, 'We'll just book somewhere else,' but I soon discovered it takes six weeks for them to reimburse the payment, even though it was their fault. We didn't have the money to just go and book another holiday so Ste and I decided we would have to miss out that year.

Obviously we were furious and, because the boys had been looking forward to going away so much, I felt terrible and Ste felt terrible. We were saying, 'What are we going to tell the boys?' But we knew there were two things they wanted more than a holiday, so we came up with a plan.

That evening, we sat them down in our living room and Ste said, 'The holiday has been cancelled. We're so sorry.' Their little faces fell. But they'd tormented us for years about getting a dog, so to soften the blow he said, 'But we've decided to buy a dog.' He paused as the boys cheered, then added, 'And we're going to get you a season ticket for Everton.'

Well, that was the best reaction to the cancellation of a holiday anyone has ever seen. The kids were made up with it. They were happier with that than they'd ever been about any holiday and, to this day, Owen says that cancelled holiday was the best thing that ever happened.

Although I had gone to games with them in the past, I didn't get a season ticket for me because I said to Ste, 'That'll be your time.' Ste worked as the night manager at Tesco and his hours meant he was out every evening during the week and the boys saw me all the time and very little of him. That made the weekends all the more precious for Ste because he loved spending time with his boys. Because of that, I wanted the matches to be Ste's time with them, so we bought three season tickets for Goodison Park. Because the kids were juniors, and Rhys was under eleven, they weren't too expensive. Less than the holiday cost anyway.

Once that was settled, we started looking for a dog. A friend who worked with Ste was mad about boxer dogs and had two beautiful boxers. She had bought them from the same breeder and she recommended him, saying he treated the dogs well. We rang him and, luckily, he said, 'I've got two dogs here. I'll bring them round.'

The following day he turned up at the house with two puppies, who were brothers, and of course Rhys wanted both of them.

'We can't have both,' I said, and luckily the breeder agreed.

'I wouldn't allow you to have two puppies anyway,' he said. 'It's too much.'

One of the puppies had a white blot on his face, which we thought was cute, so we chose him. I wanted to call him Zebedee, but because he was a boxer dog Rhys wanted to call him after heavyweight champion Lennox Lewis, so the latest addition to the family was named Lennox.

Although we never spoiled the boys, Rhys had a way of getting what he wanted out of us. He could always win me over with a cheeky grin and a pleading look – his own puppy dog eyes – and being the baby of the family meant he usually got his own way, within reason. But I was always rewarded with a look of happiness, a hug and a 'Thank you Mum,' or even a 'Love you Mum,' and that gave me a little jolt of joy, every time. If he was happy, I was happy.

Both the kids doted on that dog. Owen would get up in the middle of the night to let him in the garden for a pee and then, when he got back inside, he would sit with him for ages if he was whining, stroking him to calm him down. Personally, I am a bit wary of dogs as I was bitten by one as a child and Lennox seemed to sense that. When the kids came in through the door he would leap up and jump all over them, kissing their faces. But he could sense he shouldn't do that with me. When I came in the door, he would just look at me, like he was thinking, 'She's not into all that. She'll feed me and give me a brush but she doesn't do kisses and hugs.'

Being a boxer, Lennox was a bit of a handful, very boisterous and as he got bigger, he was very strong. When a boxer wants to go somewhere, they'll go, and he even pulled me over when I walked him round the block once. But boxers are also the jokers in the pack, making you laugh all the time – just like Rhys, in fact.

Rhys loved that dog to bits. He was always rolling around on the floor with him and couldn't wait to see him when he came home from school. They would chase each other around the house and cause a proper commotion, but their antics would always make me laugh.

Rhys's favourite treat was a Chinese meal and every September, when his birthday came round, he would choose a trip to a Chinese restaurant as his special treat. We used to say, 'Let's go somewhere different for your birthday.' But we always got the same answer, 'No. I want Chinese.'

On one holiday in Menorca, when he was still quite small, we found an all-you-can-eat Chinese buffet and Rhys was in seventh heaven. He went over to fill his own plate and came back with it piled high with nothing but crispy duck and pancake. Owen couldn't stop laughing – the meal looked almost as big as Rhys.

In July 2007, Rhys had just left primary school and was preparing to go to the secondary school, Fazakerley High School, when we went on another holiday to Menorca. We went with quite a few friends, and there were about eighteen of us, including kids. One night we were all sitting outside a bar, the kids were all getting mock cocktails and playing about and there was a pub quiz going on, so we decided to join in. We had to pick a name for the team and one of our friends picked a name that was so rude, it's almost unprintable but we did find it hilarious. It was 'Has anyone seen Mike Hunt?'

The adults were laughing so much we couldn't breathe and Rhys started laughing and laughing, even though he really didn't know what he was laughing at. It's not the sort of language he would have understood, but I think the sight of us in hysterics set him off and he was screaming with laughter. Everyone in the pub was looking at him, but he couldn't stop, and that made us laugh even more. We didn't win a prize for the quiz, but we did win a prize for the best team name!

He loved that last holiday and he had such a great time, especially round the pool. He would jump on everyone and dive-bomb everyone and just mess about all the time, trying to make people laugh. Ever the joker.

While he never stopped joking about, Rhys was always a loving lad who was always hugging and kissing me, and always throwing his arms round me. He had a wonderful smile that made you feel warm and lovely. You couldn't help but smile back at him.

Although he was growing up fast, he was still my little boy. He wouldn't have told his mates but he still liked me to come and tuck him in of a night.

Every night, Rhys would have a shower and then go to bed to read or watch a bit of telly before going to sleep. After a little while, I would go up and turn out the light and he'd say, 'Come and tuck me in,' and I'd say, 'You're nearly twelve!'

So I'd tuck him in and kiss him on the head. And every night we would say the same thing to each other.

'Love you, see you in the morning,' I'd say.

'Love you too Mum,' Rhys would reply.

What I'd give to hear those words from him one more time.

# CHAPTER TWO

# A Fateful Day

**IT MAY BE** etched in my memory for evermore now, but 22 August 2007 started like any other day. The boys had been on their school holidays for a month and Rhys had made the most of his time. Whenever he could, he had been out with a football but the summer of 2007 had seen more than its fair share of wet weather, and Rhys would often get frustrated when heavy rain stopped him from spending the whole day outside. In the few days before the 22nd, the weather had taken a turn for the better and Rhys had spent long hours at the park, or in the garden, happily kicking a football around. While he loved school, and he was excited to be going up to the secondary school, Fazakerley High School, in September, the summer holidays never felt too long for him. As long as he had a ball, he was never bored.

That day was glorious, hot and sunny, and Rhys would normally be heading straight out to knock for his mates after breakfast, but I had a day off from Tesco, where I worked on the checkouts, so I had booked dentist appointments for the boys. I took them for their check-ups and they got the all-clear, then we had to go into town. Rhys needed a smart new uniform for secondary school and I had already kitted him out with most of it, but we still had to get the tie. He had been excited to try on his new shirt, trousers and jumper, and a brand new pair of shiny black shoes, and he looked so smart. But, Rhys being Rhys, he was most excited about his new blue PE kit because it was made by Nike. He was absolutely made up that it was a decent brand and not your everyday kit. It was a proper kit. He was over the moon with that.

The school has a massive big field at the back where they play football but the pupils also do all sorts of other sports, including cricket, athletics and trampolining, as well as having the use of a swimming pool. It is quite a sporty school so Rhys was looking forward to all of the activities.

Moving to secondary school is always difficult so we occasionally had to reassure him that everything would be all right, and he'd soon settle in, but he was quite confident because he had a couple of close friends who had also got in and his big brother was in the sixth form, so it wasn't as daunting as it might have been. We were happy he was going to Fazakerley too because Ste had been there and had always rated it and Owen had done really well there.

While he loved the PE kit, I loved his spanking new uniform – grey trousers, a navy blue jumper with a badge and a new shirt and tie – when he tried it on. It all looked very smart and it brought a lump to my throat to think my baby boy was off to 'big school'.

Rhys had a football training session with Fir Tree FC that night, the first of the season, and by the time we got home from town he didn't have time to go out with his mates. Instead, he disappeared into his bedroom to play on his Xbox for a while. After an hour or so, he came down for tea and sat down with me, Ste and Owen. He only had a sandwich, because he never liked to eat a full dinner before training, then he got his blue England kit on, and off he went. Ten minutes later he was back, knocking on the door and gasping for breath.

'What are you doing back?' I asked him.

'I forgot my signing-on fee,' he said.

'Why didn't you just leave it?' I said. 'You could have paid before the match at the weekend.'

But Rhys was adamant he wanted to pay it that night so, while I went and found my purse, he went into the living room, where Ste was watching TV. He sat on the arm of the couch, panting for breath, and Ste looked at him and thought, 'He needs a haircut.' Until a few months before, he had a number two cut but he was growing it and trying to get it longer on top. We had to nag him to get it cut.

After taking a fiver out of my purse, I called Rhys out and he gave me a sheepish grin and said, 'Oh Mum, will you just run me up there because I'm going to be late now.'

The ground is only five minutes up the road so it was no bother to take him. As I dropped him off, he gave me a kiss on the cheek and said, 'Ta-ra Mum. I'll be home to watch England.' England were playing Germany that night at Wembley and he was looking forward to watching the match after practice.

After dropping him off, I came home and Ste went to work. We had both worked at Tesco for most of our working lives and as Ste was a night manager, he always set off to work after tea. He has never minded working nights – he jokes that he prefers it because he doesn't have to deal with customers. It means we can't have a social life during the week but we'd always tended to make up for it at weekends, whenever we could.

It was shortly after 7 p.m. when Ste said goodbye. Owen was in his room and I set about stripping the wallpaper off the walls in the lounge while *Coronation Street* was on the telly. I'd been wanting to spruce the room up for a while and had been bending Ste's ear about it but a few days earlier, he had put his foot down and said, 'No, we're not decorating it.' Well I wasn't having that! As soon as he'd gone out, I started stripping the walls, grinning to myself and thinking, 'We are now.'

I was just getting stuck in when there was an almighty bang at the front door. I remember thinking, 'Who the hell is that?' It was so loud the house shook. Owen rushed to the door and opened it, and there was one of Rhys's coaches, Tony, whose son was also one of Rhys's best friends.

'Is your mum there?' he asked urgently, and as I heard him, I came straight to the door. He looked shell-shocked and just said, 'You've got to come with me, now.'

'Why, what's up?' I said.

He told me Steve Geoghegan, the football manager, had just rung him and then he blurted out, 'Rhys has been shot. I don't know anything else. We just need to get up there.'

My blood ran cold and I knew there was no time to think.

I grabbed my phone and my keys and told Owen that I was going out and I'd be back in a minute, not really understanding what Tony was telling me. I don't think his words had sunk in at all, I just knew something had happened to Rhys and I had to be there. A feeling of sheer panic was rising in my chest.

As we drove I suddenly realised that I had to phone Ste. He was on the M27 motorway on the way to work in Southport when I called him and said, 'You need to come back. Rhys has been shot.'

'What?' he said, but as I went to repeat, 'Rhys has been shot,' my phone just died. I was distraught. How could I have let my phone run out of charge? How would Ste find us? Not being able to speak to Ste added to my sense of panic and fear.

Even though Tony drove as fast as he could to the Fir Tree pub, which is only minutes from the house, I couldn't get there quick enough. My boy needed me and I needed to get to him as fast as I could. As we got near, I could see hundreds of people standing in the car park, blocking my view, but I couldn't see Rhys.

What happened next was surreal. It felt like I was in a dream, or my worst nightmare, as if I wasn't really there at all. I jumped out of the car and I heard someone in the crowd say, 'Here's his mum.' At those words, the crowd magically parted to let me through and that was when I saw Rhys, lying on the floor in the middle of the car park, not moving. There was a woman hunched over him, trying to help him, and I later found out she was an off-duty nurse called Sharon Lynch, who had stepped in to try to give him first aid. She had put him in the recovery position and made sure nothing was blocking his airway.

In panic, I ran over to Rhys and knelt on the floor beside him. The crowd melted away and all I could see was my baby boy. The scene was worse than anything I had imagined or thought I would ever see. He was lying in a massive pool of blood and there was blood coming out of his mouth. His eyes were open but there was nothing there. I had no idea what to do so, instinctively, I gently cradled his head and began talking to him.

'Stay with me, Rhys,' I kept saying over and over again. 'Please stay with me. I love you.'

There was still no expression in his eyes. I was talking and talking to him, desperate to let him know I was there, but there was no flicker in his face. In hindsight, it was like he'd already gone.

As I cradled him in my arms, a young paramedic arrived and said there was an ambulance on its way but it seemed like for ever until it arrived. All the while, I kept talking to Rhys and saying, 'Stay with me, Rhys, stay with me.' I said, 'You're going to school in September. Everything is going to be all right. Stay with me, baby.'

Eventually the ambulance came and the paramedics carefully put Rhys onto a stretcher and into the back. At that point, I looked down at my white top for the first time and it was covered in blood. I'd never seen so much blood. 'How the hell could this have happened?' I asked myself. Thoughts that Rhys could actually die rushed into my head but I pushed them away. I had to cling on to the hope that a young, strong lad like Rhys could battle through anything. 'He's a fighter,' I told myself. 'He'll be fine.'

The ambulance paramedic was asking, 'Do you want to come in the ambulance or follow on?' In a daze, I climbed into the back of the ambulance, not knowing what else to do, and they asked me to sit in the back opposite Rhys.

'You'll have to put your seatbelt on,' one of the paramedics said, in a kind voice.

'No, I can't,' I said, firmly. 'It's too far away from Rhys, I won't be able to hold his hand.'

'I'm sorry,' he said. 'But we won't be able to take you if you don't.'

I had no choice, so I buckled my seatbelt. That is one thing that has always stuck in my mind. Rhys's stretcher was too far and I kept thinking, 'I don't want to have my seatbelt on. I want to be over there, beside Rhys. I want to hold his hand.' It was an added layer of torture because I couldn't reach him. I sat there stretching across and straining at the belt and I just couldn't reach, I couldn't touch him.

The medics were saying, 'He knows you're here. Just talk to him. Just keep talking to him.' All the time they were working on him and working on him, although I couldn't say what it was they were trying to do. But Rhys was just lying there, with no response,

The four-mile journey to Alder Hey Children's Hospital could only have taken about twelve minutes but it seemed eternal and was made even more agonising by the blasted speed bumps. I had never hated speed bumps so much. Every time we went over one the poor paramedics were falling over and I was beside myself, all the while thinking, 'Oh my God, why are there so many speed bumps? We need to get there quick! Why are they slowing us down?'

At the hospital, the ambulance doors opened and at least a dozen people were standing there waiting for us to arrive. They wheeled the stretcher out and ran with Rhys into the hospital and I followed, still in shock. A lady paramedic said gently, 'You need to call someone,' so, without thinking, I got the phone out of my pocket and, obviously, I still had no battery. Worse still, I couldn't remember anyone's number, not even Ste's, because you never have to physically dial numbers now everything is in your phone. The only number I could remember was my friend Carol's, who I had known for thirty-two years, since we were at primary school, and she had never changed her landline number. Because we'd been friends before we had mobiles, I'd never forgotten it.

The paramedic handed me her own phone and said, 'Phone her, and ask her to phone everyone else.'

Carol picked up straight away.

'Something terrible has happened to Rhys,' I blurted out.

'I know,' said Carol. 'A friend who was at the Fir Tree already told me. How is he?'

'I don't know,' I sobbed. 'I don't know how serious it is but he's really badly injured and we're at Alder Hey now.'

'Just tell me what you need to me do,' said Carol.

I said, 'Can you phone Ste then go to my sister's and then go to mine and tell Owen he needs to come here.'

'Of course,' she said. True to her word, she did all the running around for me. She went and got my sister, Debra, and got Owen and brought them to the hospital.

Rhys was taken straight into the trauma room and instantly surrounded by a host of doctors and nurses. His blue England football top, now dark red and soaked through with blood, was carefully cut off him by one of the nurses. Then she unlaced his football boots, still caked in mud, and peeled off his long football socks and put them carefully in a plastic bag with the rest of his clothes. They were taken off for forensics along with his football bag and even a bottle of Lucozade he'd been drinking at football training. There was still no reaction from Rhys, and no flicker of life, and seeing him lying there, while I was powerless to help, was torment. I was beside myself with fear and distress.

By the time Ste turned up, thirty minutes after I called him, I was both distraught and furious. I was screaming, 'Where have you been? Why have you taken this long?' But it wasn't his fault at all.

Ste hadn't known which hospital we were at and had gone to Fazakerley instead of Alder Hey. His first thought, he told me later, was that Rhys had been shot with an air rifle or air pistol. When Ste was a kid air guns were quite popular and he remembered a lad at school getting shot with one when they were playing football. Even so, he could tell from my voice that it was serious enough to turn straight round and head back.

Not knowing where we were, Ste had headed towards the training ground where the team had football practice on Wednesday nights. There's only one road on and off our estate and, as he turned in, he saw an ambulance speed past him, but he had no way of knowing Rhys and I were inside. At the Fir Tree, he saw the crowd in the car park and so he stopped there. By the time he arrived the car park had been cordoned off by police and there were a lot of people milling around, so he got out of the car and looked over to the car park and he could see the blood on the floor. Suddenly, Ste realised that it might be even more serious than he had thought, and he began to panic.

He heard someone say, 'They've taken him to hospital,' so naturally he assumed they had taken him to the nearest hospital at Fazakerley, and that's where he went next. Ste rushed into A&E and asked the staff if a little boy had been brought in and they obviously knew about it, because they immediately told him Rhys was at Alder Hey Children's Hospital, on the other side of the city, a twenty-minute drive away. He jumped back in the car and, now desperate to get to us, drove as fast as he could, his panic increasing with every red light and traffic queue he came across.

As soon as he got to Alder Hey, and walked through the double doors into the trauma department, Ste found me outside the relatives' room, opposite the trauma room where Rhys lay. I just kept saying, 'They can't resuscitate him. They can't resuscitate him,' over and over again. Having had no information at all up to that point, Ste was still assuming Rhys had been hit by a pellet gun, fired by some silly kid mucking around. Because we don't move in circles where guns are prevalent, it hadn't crossed his mind that a proper firearm was involved.

Ste put his arms round me and I tried to explain what was happening, but I was incoherent with panic, so I don't know if I was making much sense.

The scene at the hospital just felt surreal. It felt like I was there, but not there. We were in the middle of absolute chaos, with frantic activity going on around us and around Rhys, and it was impossible to take it all in. I was left bemused, thinking, 'What's this all about? How can this be happening?'

Soon after Ste arrived, we were taken through to the trauma room where they were still working on Rhys, and the doctor explained to Ste what was going on. As soon as he saw Rhys and the doctor said 'He's been shot with a gun,' Ste suddenly realised how serious this was and the colour drained from his face.

Rhys was lying on a stretcher in the middle of the room. The blue blood-soaked shirt that he'd been wearing when he first went into the trauma room had now gone and they had also taken off his shorts because he had tubes going into his groin and his arms. There were monitors and wires attached all over him, a heart monitor next to the table and an X-ray machine that was showing live X-rays on the screen. There were countless doctors and nurses around him – so many people. It's hard to comprehend just how many people were working on my little boy and he looked so young and vulnerable, lying there. My arms longed to reach out and give him a cuddle, tell him it would be all right, just as I had when he was a tiny boy and had hurt himself by falling off his bike or falling over and grazing his knee. But how could I tell him it was going to be fine when I didn't know he was going to get through this at all?

While they worked as a team, there was one surgeon who stood apart from them, giving orders and telling people what to do. The nurse who had taken Rhys's football boots and socks off asked us to stand at the end of the bed.

'Rub his feet, tell him he'll be OK, and just keep talking to him,' the surgeon told us. Rhys's feet felt cold to the touch and as I was rubbing them, I was looking at him lying there fighting for his life, surrounded by all these strangers. There was blood everywhere, running on the table and dripping onto the floor. It was horrendous.

The surgeon was saying, 'We're going to try this ...' Then he'd say, 'That's not working, we're going to try something else.' None of it was really going in and Ste and I were just nodding. Then he said, 'That's not working. We only have one other option and if that doesn't work, there's no other option.' But even at that point, I still wasn't fully taking in the extent of what was happening.

After a few minutes he looked at us and shook his head sadly, and just said, 'No.' Then he said, 'Can everybody stand back.' Suddenly, the enormity of the situation sank in and I completely lost it. I started shouting, 'No, no, carry on. You can't stop.' I ran to the top of the table, looking at my darling boy with all these tubes in him, covered in blood, his hair all matted.

'You've got to keep going,' I demanded.

The doctor shook his head and said, 'I'm sorry. There's nothing else we could do.'

He explained that Rhys's heart wouldn't beat on its own and they couldn't find where the bleed was coming from. The surgeon was really calm. He knew exactly what he was doing and everyone in that room listened to him, so he was clearly a great trauma surgeon, but he just couldn't save Rhys. I couldn't believe what I was hearing. It was the most horrendous thing a parent can ever hear, and it was happening to us.

Rhys was declared dead at 8.46 p.m. Just an hour and a half before that he'd been in goal, at the training session, and fielding penalties, getting miffed because his coach, Steve, got one past him. Now he was gone for ever.

The doctors and nurses all cleared the room and we were just standing there, in shock. The surgeon said, 'Do you want to go to the relatives' room while we take the tubes out?' I was still in a daze. The relatives' room was just opposite the operating theatre and by this time most of our family were in there – Owen, my brothers and sister, Ste's brothers.

As soon as we walked in they all chorused, 'Is he all right? Is he all right?' My niece, who was a nurse at the hospital, was there and, ignoring the barrage of questions, I walked blindly over to her and begged for her help.

'You need to go out there because they told me he's dead and I don't believe it,' I said. 'You need to go out and check. If you tell me I'll believe it. I don't believe them.'

She put her arms round me and said, 'Mel, you have to believe them. He's gone. He's dead.' I was just hysterical, absolutely hysterical. This just couldn't be true. I refused to believe it.

After a few minutes of me crying hysterically, while Ste put his arms round me and tried to comfort me, the surgeon came and called us back in, but this time we all came in and we stood round the bed in stunned silence. The eerie silence in the room was a huge contrast to the frantic chaos moments before, with monitors bleeping, doctors shouting and everyone battling to save our child's life. Now there was nothing to say and no more that could be done.

As we held hands around the bed, weeping and shocked, the hospital chaplain came in and started praying over Rhys, asking God to take him into his arms and all that religious stuff. Although I was brought up a Catholic, and Ste is Church of England, neither of us are churchgoers and at that point, the words meant nothing to me. If there was a God, I thought, how could this be happening? Even then, even after they'd told us he'd gone, it wasn't properly sinking in. We were all just standing there looking at each other, holding each other's hands and none of us had a clue what to do next. It was as if we were all waiting for someone to tell us they'd got it wrong or give us some instructions.

Eventually, after about twenty minutes, they asked us all to leave. Our families started to drift away but I wouldn't go home. I couldn't. I was still hysterical.

'I'm not leaving him here,' I told them. 'I'm not going home, I'm not. I'm just not doing it.' I was causing a bit of a scene but I didn't care.

'You've got to go home,' they kept telling me, but I absolutely refused. I just couldn't leave my little boy there alone.

After a while there was just me, Ste and Rhys left in the room, Ste and I still too stunned to speak. A member of staff came over to talk to us and they said, 'If you want to wait for half an hour, we will get Rhys to the morgue and you can go and see him there.'

'I'll wait,' I said, straight away. Anything rather than leave and go home. Looking back, I was probably being naïve but I thought I would be able to give him a cuddle once he was there. I was aching to hug him. So I thought, 'Once he gets to the morgue, I'll be able to give him a hug and tell him I love him.' However, even that turned out to be impossible.

By now it was getting late so, when we got the summons, we walked through the dark hospital grounds to the mortuary, still numb from shock. But when we got there Rhys was behind glass, lying on a trolley, and I could only look at him. They were saying, 'You can't go in. Come back tomorrow and see him.' The physical need to cuddle him was so strong it was eating me up inside, so to look and not be able to touch was devastating. His surroundings looked so cold and clinical that the thought of leaving him there alone was truly traumatic.

Ste gently led me away and back to the car. Somehow he managed to drive home.

By the time we got back, it was about midnight. Walking through the front door, without Rhys, I almost felt I should shout up to his room, tell him we were home, as I had done a million times before. But he couldn't hear me now and there would be no cheerful 'Hi Mum' in response. It was too much to bear.

The three of us – me, Ste and Owen – walked silently upstairs and sat on Rhys's bed, on his Everton duvet, surrounded by his football posters and trophies, in a state of total shock. We kept saying, 'I don't understand this. What's happened?' We just didn't know what to say. There were just no words. We looked at each other in disbelief. We were all totally incapable of comprehending this terrible situation. We just couldn't understand that he was dead.

None of us slept at all that night. Unable to leave Rhys's bedroom, I climbed into his bed and pulled the duvet over me, but it wasn't because I thought I could get any sleep. It would be years before I would have a proper night's sleep again.

# CHAPTER THREE

# A Long Goodbye

**THE NEXT MORNING,** shattered from lack of sleep and still numb with shock, I felt completely lost. I couldn't think about anything other than getting back to the hospital to be with Rhys. I couldn't eat breakfast, couldn't think past that morning and couldn't even begin to comprehend what had led to our lovely, innocent eleven-year-old, who had kissed me goodbye just twelve hours before, lying in a morgue.

Before we could go back, though, we had been told the police would be coming to see us, first thing. And, early that morning, there was a knock on the door and there was Dave Kelly, the detective who was running the murder investigation, and the two family liaison officers (FLOs) who were assigned to our case, who we will call Jenny and John (not their real names) out of respect for their privacy. They wanted to talk to us but I only had one thing on my mind.

'I don't even want to know what's going on,' I told them. 'I just need to go and see him.'

At this point we hadn't been officially told anything about what had happened. We'd been told rumours, things my family had heard and had told us at the hospital, but not the actual sequence of events. That wasn't what mattered. I just wanted to get back to Rhys as fast as I could.

Dave introduced himself and said he'd been given the job of investigating the shooting and that he was going to do his utmost to solve it and bring the people responsible to justice. He was in his forties, smartly dressed in a suit, with closely cropped grey hair. We could tell straight away that he was a proper scouser, with an open, honest manner and, while he was sympathetic and full of condolences, he would be someone who told it how it was. Somehow, we trusted him immediately.

He said, 'I can't bring Rhys back but I won't stop until I put the people responsible behind bars.' He offered to get the FLOs to run me, Ste and Owen to the hospital but first he wanted to talk to us and tell us what had gone on.

As well as filling us in on the actual events of the night before, Dave wanted to know about us as a family, and about Owen. They had been wondering if there was a connection between Owen and the Croxteth Crew, or Crocky Crew, a local gang known for violent attacks, but any suspicion of that was quickly quashed. They could see that Rhys wouldn't have been involved in anything like that. We were pretty shocked but we could see they needed to ask the question. They told us they still thought this was a gang-related incident but, to be honest, none of it was sinking in, I was in such a state.

We had had no real dealings with the police before this and we had no idea how this all worked, but as soon as we met Dave we just knew he was going to get a result. We knew he was a local and he came across as passionate and determined, He was very keen to reassure us, as much as he could. He kept saying, 'We will sort this. We will catch them.' But he had a warning for us too.

'Don't be listening to anything that gets floated about,' he said. 'Don't read anything on social media because it will be rubbish. If you've got any questions, ask me. If you have any worries, ask me.' He said the FLOs were there to help and we should ask them if we needed anything.

Although he told us the outline of what had happened, Dave didn't give us any details about the shooting. It was early days and I suppose there was that much information coming in, they had to sift out what was real and what wasn't.

Dave also asked if he could have a photo of Rhys, to help with the inquiry and also to release to the press. Ste looked through our recent holiday photos and gave him two. There's one where Rhys is sitting down and another where he's leaning forward with a red background – in both he's wearing football shirts, of course. They were the first photos that came to hand in the chaos and they are not his best ones. It never crossed our minds how widely those pictures would be circulated in the media, and how familiar the images would become to everyone around the country. After a while I began to think that those images of Rhys was all people saw but he wasn't just about those photos and there was a lot more to him.

As Dave left I grabbed hold of his hands and looked up at him and said, 'Please, please, get them. Just get them.' Dave squeezed my hands back, looked me straight in the face and, in a quiet voice, filled with sincerity, he said, 'I will.'

The FLOs drove me, Ste and Owen to the mortuary and Jenny came in with us. Rhys had been washed, although he was still behind the glass screen. The difference was that overnight some kind hospital worker – and we still don't know who it was – had put him under an Everton duvet, with an Everton pillow. We were told he had gone out and bought it to make the room look more like Rhys's bedroom and it was an exact copy of the bedding he had at home, so he looked like he was asleep in his own bed. I longed to cuddle him. I turned to Jenny.

'I need to go in and see him,' I said. 'I have to go in.'

'If you go in, I'm afraid it is going to be really difficult for you as you are not allowed to touch him,' she said.

'Fine,' I said. 'Just let me go in.' I wasn't really listening to her, to be honest, and I just had to get closer to my boy. Walking through that door, I felt sick to the bottom of my stomach and the agony actually felt physical. I couldn't believe my son, the little boy who had kissed me goodbye just yesterday, was lying in a hospital mortuary.

Not surprisingly, Owen had only been in the room for a couple of minutes when the whole thing got too much for him and he said, 'Mum, I can't do this.'

'You go,' I said. 'That's fine.' He was still a young lad himself, just seventeen, and it must have been totally overwhelming for him, so I would never force him to stay. I was worried about how Owen would cope but at that moment, I knew I had to let him handle it the best way he could while Ste and I processed what had happened. We would just have to be there to support him when he needed us to.

Owen went outside and Ste and I sat with Rhys, with Jenny watching us from the end of the bed.

Rhys liked to have his hair styled in a certain way. Since he'd had it longer on top he had always gelled it because he liked it to stick up. Although they had washed his hair, which had been matted with blood the night before, I knew he wouldn't like the way it looked as he was lying there. I wanted to get it to stick up, so I reached out to try to fix it the best I could, then I gave him a little kiss on the head, as I had so often done when he was tucked up in bed at home.

Behind me, Jenny said firmly, 'Do not touch him.'

I stood still, shocked. Quietly, I said, 'I'm just giving him a kiss and fixing his hair.'

'Do it again, and I'm going to arrest you,' she said, without a hint of compassion. She was standing at the foot of the bed and I turned my head to look at her, thinking, 'You heartless cow.'

Ste took one look at me and grabbed hold of me, because he could see that I was on the verge of losing it. I was clearly upset and he knew it.

'Come on,' he said. 'Let's go.' He put his arms round me and dragged me out.

I was fuming and the whole thing made matters so much worse that day. It was like he wasn't mine, he was evidence and I couldn't contaminate it. It was ridiculous. He was my son and my DNA was all over him. I'd given him a hug before he went to football and he kissed me as he got out of the car. Surely, I thought, you can eliminate my DNA on my own son so I can give him one last cuddle.

Bad news travels fast and I didn't have to tell anyone about Rhys's death. Everybody knew. It was all over the news, Facebook and other social media and Ste's mum, Doreen, who hadn't been able to get to the hospital, found out Rhys was dead from the television news. Ste had called her to say Rhys had been shot before he dashed to the hospital, but she hadn't known how serious it was until she turned on the TV and, with the speed of modern media, we hadn't had a chance to tell her before it was reported all over the country. We felt terrible she'd heard it that way but the events of the night before had been so traumatic that there had been no chance to call her before the media report went out. We called as soon as we could and, of course, she was heartbroken.

After we left Alder Hey, Dave Kelly asked us to hold a press conference to appeal for witnesses, and anyone who knew about the shooting, to come forward. We were still in a state of total shock and I wasn't sure what I could say but Dave told us that the first few days were crucial when it came to the investigation and said that, as the shooting was on the front page of all the national newspapers and the top item on TV and radio news, it would really help them if we could make the appeal as soon as we could.

Sitting in front of a room of strangers, to talk about how I had found Rhys bleeding in the car park, was really traumatic. I was in pieces and Ste, sitting beside me with his arm round me the whole time, was as strong as anyone could be.

Between sobs, I told them what had happened and how I had held Rhys in my arms as his life slipped away.

'Our son was only eleven,' I said. 'He was just a baby. This shouldn't have happened. This shouldn't be going on. Please help us. The whole family is devastated. We've lost our world.

'People know, someone knows who's done it and I know people must be frightened to come forward but we cannot leave the killer who did this out on the streets.

'The same thing could happen to someone else. It could be their son next time. It will happen again.

'My baby boy, he was only eleven. He didn't deserve this. He's never allowed out late and he has to be inside by 8.30 p.m. His older brother Owen never goes out or hangs out in gangs. Rhys was only eleven. How would he even know about that?'

Although he likes to keep his feelings to himself, Ste has a way with words and he probably put it best when he told the journalists, 'We're devastated. We've lost our world and the world has lost a good guy.'

The whole press conference was over in minutes but it was hugely traumatic and harrowing so soon after losing Rhys. I understood why it had to be done but I just wanted to shut myself away from the world and try to come to terms with the massive loss in our lives in peace. My only hope was that our words would bring people out of the woodwork so we could find out who had taken our baby boy away from us and get justice for Rhys.

As word spread, people soon began flocking to the house. We had such a houseful we had to go out and buy loads more mugs for the endless cups of tea and use garden chairs for people to sit on. People were in the house, in the garden, everywhere. For the most part, they didn't know what to say or do – they just knew they wanted to be here, which was understandable.

Owen, who is a quiet lad anyway, found it really hard. He was in his room constantly and he wouldn't come down. He didn't like having so many people in the house, some of whom he didn't even know, so he kept out of their way.

One day when someone he did not recognise called, he asked 'Who are they? When was the last time they came to see you? What are they doing here now?'

'Owen,' I said. 'You have to understand that sometimes life gets in the way. You're working and you're bringing up families and you say to yourself, "I must go and see them," but you get too busy. Just because they haven't seen Rhys for a while doesn't mean they haven't thought about him.'

But he wasn't happy having a houseful, and he was the same at the funeral. He kept saying, 'Who are all these people? Why are they here?' That's very much

Owen's character. He has no time for people who haven't got time to make an effort and visit and he's a very loyal lad. He had a close group of friends at school and they are still his friends. I understand exactly how he felt but everyone has their own lives. I do it myself. I think 'I must phone so-and-so' but by the time I get home from work, and have my tea, I look at my watch and it's nine-thirty in the evening, and I think, 'It's a bit late to phone now.' That's life. But Owen couldn't comprehend any of that.

It wasn't just when the house was full that Owen hid away. He didn't want to talk about it, at all, and he just stayed in his room the whole time. He wouldn't even come down for his tea most nights. I would take something up to his room and I'd sit on the end of his bed, and try to chat. But I think it took him a long time to truly understand that Rhys wasn't coming back.

From the night we came home from the hospital, we had a police car outside the house, and an officer often stood on the drive, to keep any unwanted visitors away. In the early days the FLOs were there every day, all day, because there was so much to take in, and so much to be explained to us, as to what goes on in the wake of a child's murder and what we could and couldn't do.

On one occasion, Ste told them, 'I need to go out. I need to get petrol.'

'No you can't go and get petrol,' said John. 'What do you need the car for anyway? You're not going anywhere.'

Of course he was right and we could have faced a crowd of reporters had we ventured out. There were even a couple of times when Owen was pictured walking the dog around the block, because he still needed a walk, and Ste took him out at five in the morning to avoid being seen. But, even though we were keen to hide away and had no desire to go out, the fact that we were unable to leave the house even if we wanted to took some getting used to.

After a couple of days Tony, the breeder we had bought the dog from, phoned us and said, 'Do you want me to take Lennox off your hands for a couple of weeks while you get things sorted?' We had the funeral to arrange and there was a lot going on so we thought it was best that Lennox went and stayed there for a while. Tony always looked after him when we went abroad anyway and, as long as we provided the food and bought a bottle of duty-free, he didn't charge us. It gave him an opportunity to bring in a different blood line into his breeding, because Lennox was all still 'intact.' A holiday for Lennox seemed a good idea, given that we were unable to walk him freely.

To be honest, the press were pretty good about leaving us alone at home. Dave always used to say that the press could be real a-holes but they could also be real diamonds when it came to getting information out there that might just bring someone forward. They are a useful tool and 99 per cent of them are decent people, doing a job. You only get the odd ones who are idiots.

During that time, I refused to look at any social media and I stopped watching the news, in case there was a mention of Rhys. Occasionally, if Ste hadn't heard anything for a while, he'd say, 'I'm just putting the news on for a minute,' but he'd turn it off very quickly so I didn't have to listen to it.

Personally, I didn't want any distractions. Although I was absolutely distraught I just wanted to stay totally focused and be completely lucid. Every day was a huge challenge. I couldn't function normally, I didn't know what day of the week it was and I struggled to put food on the table for any of us. I totally fell apart.

Ste would say to me, 'Let's just get through the next hour, then we'll worry about the hour after that.' That became our mantra and the only way to live. If Dave was coming over in two hours' time, with an update, we would say, 'Let's just make it through until Dave gets here.' We couldn't think as far as teatime, or tomorrow. We were literally living hour by hour.

My friends, and especially my sister, Debra, were constantly at the house and they worried about me. They would say, 'You need to eat. You need to sleep.' But I told them, 'I don't need to do anything. I just want to know what's going on.'

Many of my friends and family suggested I go to the doctor's, insisting that I needed sleeping tablets and sedatives, but I was adamant. 'No, I won't,' I told them. 'I want to be totally aware of what's going on. I don't want anyone making decisions without me.' Later, at the funeral, my doctor approached me and offered me sleeping pills, and I still refused.

Despite the immense pain I was feeling in the days after Rhys's death, which was almost unbearable, I just knew I didn't want to be numb. I didn't want to be groggy or unaware of what was going on. This was something that was major, and that happened in my life, and I didn't want to be in a daze. I didn't want anyone to be whispering and saying, 'Shh, don't tell her, it might upset her,' even with the best intentions. I have to know what is going on because that is the way I deal with things. I've always been like that. Nothing I could do would bring my Rhys back but at least I could be in control of what happened next.

When the first flood of well-wishers came to the house to visit, they were only offered tea or coffee, and no alcohol, as Ste and I both felt we needed to have clear heads in case any news came in.

One of the people who came round to see us in the early days was Rhys's coach Steve, who had been the last person to see him that night. He told us that he had offered Rhys a lift home and Rhys had said no, he wanted to walk. Just minutes later, Steve and his son Sean were driving past the pub car park when Sean suddenly screamed Rhys's name and Steve turned round and saw him hit the floor. He didn't hear any shots, or see a gunman, but he stopped the car and both of them raced straight over to Rhys, before calling an ambulance and sending Tony to get me from home. Hearing about Rhys's last minutes, in this detail, was horrific and I broke down, once more, in tears.

Steve said that he felt terrible for not making Rhys take the offer of a lift home, but we told him it was not his fault. It was broad daylight and Rhys had walked that way hundreds of times before. There was no way anyone would have thought he was in danger that night.

Everyone coming to the house told us that the Fir Tree car park was filling up with flowers, messages and tributes to Rhys. A couple of days after he died, we were persuaded to go down to take a look.

It was a traumatic, distressing moment for me. When I'd seen that sort of thing on the TV, I'd always thought, 'Why do people do that? Why do they go and see the flowers?' But when it happened to us, family and friends told us, 'You need to go and see the tributes.' In the end we went because it meant publicity, which could help with the police investigation, but it was totally overwhelming.

When we got there, we were shocked to see a huge crowd of reporters and photographers who were being kept back by a police cordon. We were led to the pile of flowers, signed shirts, football boots and tributes to Rhys, all piled on a grass verge at the side of the car park. There was a huge Winnie the Pooh teddy bear in an Everton strip, and notes from all of Rhys's friends, who had brought a teddy bear and flowers. Some of them had been to nursery and primary school with him and were going on to Fazakerley with him too, and they'd left really touching tributes. I knelt down, sobbing as I read as many as I could, but I couldn't read them all because there were just too many there.

We left our own flowers at the scene with a message that read, 'Goodnight God bless son, till we meet again. All our love and kisses. From Mum, Dad & Owen. XXXXX'

While Ste and I attempted to come to terms with Rhys's shooting and deal with our private pain, an extraordinary thing was happening in Liverpool. News of the murder had united the city in grief. A local radio station called a gun amnesty and the *Liverpool Echo* launched a charity in memory of Rhys. Even Everton and Liverpool FC football clubs, mired in decades of rivalry, united to back the campaign. A petition to ask the government to crack down on gun crime received thousands of signatures from around the country.

Outside of Liverpool, the Prime Minister, Gordon Brown, held a crime summit at Number 10 and called the shooting a 'heinous crime that shocked the whole of the country'.

David Cameron, who was Conservative leader at the time, said, 'We have had a spate of children killing children, and we have got to ask what's going wrong in the country?'

Everton FC, knowing that Rhys was a devoted fan, were particularly supportive. The first team squad, including Rhys's favourites Joleon Lescott, Joseph Yobo, Mikel Arteta, Tim Cahill and Andy Johnson, visited the pub car park where Rhys had been shot and held a minute's silence. They left a blue and white football made from flowers and signed shirts and boots and Arteta left his shirt with the message 'See you in heaven' handwritten in the number six.

The captain, Phil Neville, made a short speech and appealed for people to help catch the killer.

'We all feel very sad,' he said. 'We are here today to pay our respects and appeal to anyone to come out and give information about the person who did this terrible thing.

'Rhys was an eleven-year-old lad and massive Evertonian. We just hope this thing never happens again.'

Three days after he died, they held a minute's applause before a home game against Blackburn Rovers at Goodison Park, and invited us to be there.

The minute's applause was actually our idea. Initially the club told us they were going to have a minute's silence but I didn't want that. 'Rhys was never quiet for a moment,' I said. 'So why remember him with a minute's silence?'

Before we arrived at the ground we met Harry Ross, Everton's chaplain, at St Luke the Evangelist, the church next to the ground. He showed us the book of condolence that had been set up and signed by hundreds of people, and the many candles that had been lit for Rhys. As soon as we walked in Harry held out his arms to me and gave me a warm hug.

'You will never get over this but you will find a way to deal with it,' he said. I was shocked that he was so honest and upfront, not trying to give me false hope, but I was also grateful that he avoided meaningless platitudes.

After the meeting with Harry, we went to the ground where we were taken to meet Bill Kenwright, the club's chairman, before going on to the pitch for the one minute's applause. I don't remember much more about that day. I remember standing on the pitch, holding hands with Owen and Ste, while 38,000 fans gave the minute's applause. We stood with David Moyes, the Everton manager, and then we were taken to the director's box for the match but most of it passed in a blur.

All the players for both Everton and Blackburn wore black armbands in honour of Rhys, and the Blackburn team presented us with a bouquet of flowers that was so big we could barely get it in the car. When we got home, we took it into the house but it was that big, I didn't really want it in the living room.

'Do you want me to take it up to the Fir Tree?' said Owen. 'All the other football team tributes are up there.' I thought that was a good idea so Owen got his mates to come round and they carried it up between them and laid it with all the others. It was an emotional moment for him but I was really proud of how composed he was, especially as he was being photographed by the press at the site, which would have been difficult for him.

Eventually the council would tell us they had to move all the flowers and shirts, which was perfectly understandable, so they got in touch to ask us what we wanted to do with the shirts. I said I didn't want them but Debra said, 'You might want them in the future.' She went and collected them and brought them home, and because they had been outside in all sorts of weather, she washed them all and put them in her loft, where most of them still are today.

I did take three back – shirts signed by Yobo, Arteta and Johnson – because they were Rhys's favourites. Later on, I took them and got them framed and they are still hanging in the house.

Despite their traditional rivalry with Everton, Liverpool FC did their bit too. We got a call from their chief executive Rick Parry saying that at their next match they wanted to play the tune 'Johnny Todd', better known as the theme from *Z Cars*, which is the Everton theme and the tune our players run out to at the beginning of a game. They asked us to come to Anfield for the tribute on 30 August, before a match against Toulouse.

To be honest, the prospect of the Liverpool game was much scarier to me than the Goodison Park game. Obviously, I knew everyone at Everton was on our side, and would be right behind the tribute to Rhys. But there is a lot of bitter rivalry between the two clubs, both then and now, and this was the first time the theme would have been played at Anfield. Although Rick Parry said that many of the fans had requested it, there were also a lot of Liverpool supporters who were absolutely fuming. They didn't want it played there and thought it was sacrilege, so there was a lot of conflict over the decision. Because of that, I admit, I really didn't want to go.

The FLOs drove us to that match and came in with us. We were in a normal car rather than a police car and, as we drew into the car park at Anfield, I said to Ste, 'I hope they don't say anything,' because I was really apprehensive. I needn't have worried. As soon as I got out I felt Liverpool supporters tapping me on the back and patting my shoulder in support and I relaxed a bit.

'I think it's going to be OK,' I said to Ste.

When we got into the ground there was a minute's applause again, and they did play the *Z Cars* theme – not all of it, but they played it – and that will probably be the only time that ever happens. Rhys would have loved that so much. It was a very emotional moment.

It wasn't just Liverpool that was touched by our loss. We had letters and cards from all over the world – Australia, Japan, Canada, America. Our poor postman was turning up with sackful after sackful of letters and cards and in the end got himself a big trolley so he could wheel the sacks up the path. I had to apologise to him for us receiving so much mail and, with all that was going on, we just had to open the garage door and throw all the bags in until we had time to read them.

Even so, we were grateful that people took the time to write to us.

It took a few days for Rhys's body to be released from the hospital. The coroner for Liverpool, André Rebello, said they would release the body as soon as they could but because it was a murder investigation it would take longer. For legal reasons, in a murder case, the other side has the right to their own post-mortem to gain any information that might be relevant to their case. But if no charges have been brought by the time of the autopsy, as in our case, they do a second, independent autopsy to ensure that the findings are consistent. He promised he would hurry up the process so that they could release Rhys back to us, but it was an agonising wait, not being able to see my little boy, and it seemed especially cruel that we had to put up with them treating him as evidence. I couldn't bear to think what they were putting his body through.

As soon as he was released from hospital, following the post-mortem, he was taken to a funeral parlour on the other side of Liverpool. Because of the glare of publicity the shooting had attracted, the funeral director, Barry Coyne, advised us not to use a funeral parlour anywhere close to the house.

'I know it sounds awful,' he explained, in a kind voice. 'But because this is all over the papers people you don't know might try to get in to see Rhys. Even the people involved in the shooting could turn up. It would be better if he could be laid out somewhere across town.' The thought that those scumbags would come anywhere near him again was shocking but if there was any possibility of that we had to stop it, so we agreed.

As soon as we were allowed to go to the funeral parlour, the FLOs took us to see him. The parlour staff were playing a CD with all the Everton songs, including Rhys's favourite All Together Now, which was really thoughtful, and they led us through to the room where Rhys lay. He had his Everton football kit on and they'd gelled his hair so it stuck up, just the way he liked it. He had a little bit of tinted lip balm on so his lips didn't look blue and he did actually look like he was asleep. Looking at that boyish face that I loved so much, looking the way I'd seen him when he was sleeping a million times before, was too much. I broke down and sobbed and sobbed. I was inconsolable.

We didn't stay too long on the first occasion because they said he couldn't be 'out of the fridge' for too long, which was a terrible thought for us. Owen didn't want to go to the funeral parlour, because he thought it would be too hard to see his brother like that, so the last time Owen saw Rhys was at Alder Hey. But Ste and I went there every day until we were allowed to bring him home, just three days before the funeral.

Because of what the funeral director had said, we left specific instructions that only close friends and family could see Rhys at the parlour and if anyone tried to visit him, they should ring us to check that we knew them. In the end, nobody turned up who shouldn't have been there, probably because they didn't know where he was. If he'd been near our house, it might have been a different story.

Barry, the funeral director, was a very kind man and he told me, 'Try to remember the happy eleven years you had with Rhys and not the years you won't.' It was good advice, although I was too distraught to hear it at the time.

After a day or two, I wanted to bring Rhys home because I knew he was ready but Barry, drawing on his wealth of experience with the bereaved, told me, 'You need to get yourself sorted first.'

'No,' I said. 'I want him home.'

'Yes, I know,' he said, gently. 'I'm going to bring him home, I promise, but have you got your clothes ready for the funeral? Have you got something you can wear?'

I shook my head. 'Well, in that case you need to go off and buy something because I can guarantee you that once I bring Rhys home, you won't leave his side. So get yourself organised and then I'll bring him home.' It turned out he was right.

Taking his advice, I called Debra, and she took me to the shopping centre. I bought a plain black suit and rang the funeral director to tell him I was ready. The next day Rhys came home.

Before Rhys left the parlour, we had to start sorting out the funeral arrangements. Originally, we were going to choose a plain white coffin but Barry said, 'I know a place that does football-themed caskets,' and we instantly thought that would say much more about Rhys than a plain one. Owen had his reservations, though.

'But it's got to look proper, Mum,' he said firmly, as soon as I mentioned it. 'It's got to look right otherwise it's going to look stupid.'

'OK,' I said. 'I'll get them to email me a picture of it and if you don't think it looks right, we'll get the white one.'

As soon as the email came, Owen looked it over and he said, 'That looks all right. Yeah, that's fine.' So Rhys would have his Everton coffin – royal blue at the top with a sky-blue line at the bottom and the Everton badge on the side.

We always involved Owen in every decision we made, both in the immediate aftermath and as time went on. Rhys was his little brother and I wouldn't want to do anything without consulting him, and that hasn't changed to this day.

When Rhys was due to come home, we didn't want to have an open casket so we had the lid on, although it wasn't screwed on. We laid Rhys out in the lounge along the back wall, where I could keep an eye on him from the couch. That evening, and the three nights that followed, I didn't go to bed at all because I just couldn't bear to leave Rhys down in the living room on his own. I had to be with him until we said our final goodbye.

Arranging the funeral proved more difficult than even I had imagined. Stuck in my bubble of grief,

I hadn't realised that anyone other than us and our friends and family would feel deeply affected by Rhys's death and, while I'd been told what was going on, I hadn't really understood what an impact it had had on the whole city. When the FLOs came over to talk about the funeral, I was still imagining a small local ceremony.

'There's a nice little church right beside Rhys's school,' I told them. 'We're thinking about having it there.'

'I'm afraid you can't have it there,' said Jenny.

'Why can't I have it there?' I said, defiantly.

'Because it won't be able to take the number of people that will turn up,' she said.

'There's only going to be us, the rest of the family and a few friends,' I insisted. 'There won't be that many people turning up.'

'Believe me,' she said. 'There are going to be a lot of people turning up. It needs to be in the cathedral. It needs to be organised because there is going to be loads of people. We need the police to monitor the roads, we need security.'

I was dumbfounded. I was thinking, 'This is my son's funeral! I don't understand that.' But it was decided that it would have to be at Liverpool Cathedral, the Anglican cathedral that towers over the centre of the city, and that was taken out of our hands.

Once we had agreed to the cathedral, it all began to feel a bit too political. Everyone had their ideas about how things should be done and we were just expected to adhere to that, even if it wasn't really what we wanted. It felt like we didn't have much say in it and it seemed a bit impersonal, like it wasn't about Rhys so much as being about what everyone else wanted.

The police also explained that we should let the press have access to the funeral, as it would increase exposure and could help in the investigation. The hope was that it would increase the influx of information as people saw it on TV and in the papers, and reacted. When they had got what they wanted, the police advised us, we would have the opportunity to have a private burial.

The Bishop of Liverpool, the Right Reverend James Jones, came to see us at home to discuss the order of service and choose the hymns. He was an impressive character, very intelligent, but he was also very sympathetic and tried to put us at our ease. Even so, it was clear we weren't going get everything we wanted for the funeral.

Ste said he wanted the hymn 'Guide Me O Thou Great Redeemer' but the bishop told him, 'I'm afraid you can't have that in a Church of England cathedral. That's more of a Catholic hymn.'

Both Ste and I were upset by that. Surely we should be able to have whatever hymn we wanted at our son's funeral. But Ste stayed silent and just shot me an exasperated look.

'How about "All Things Bright and Beautiful"?' said Ste.

'Yes, you can have that,' said the bishop. 'We'll let you have that one.' So that's what we had.

On top of all the cathedral arrangements, there were all the people and VIPs who wanted to come along and we also had to accommodate the press, who were taking a huge interest. It all began to feel like a massive circus.

In the end there were 2,500 people at Rhys's funeral. I know it shows the city in a good light and people were reaching out to us because they felt for us. I understand all that and we were comforted by the outpouring of support. But on the flip side we just wanted to say goodbye to our boy with a quiet funeral, surrounded by people who loved him. That was not to be. As the police told us, 'You were never going to have a quiet funeral. It's not going to happen.'

One thing that was entirely our choice was the dress code. Ste and I discussed what everyone should wear and decided that Rhys would have wanted everyone in football shirts, so we started off with the idea that people could wear any football shirt – not just Everton, because some of his friends were Liverpool supporters too. Then we decided to tell people that if they didn't want to wear a football shirt they could wear something bright. Before settling on anything, though, we asked Owen for his opinion and he thought it was a great idea, so we stuck with it. I didn't want everybody dressed in black and making it too sombre an occasion, because that's not what Rhys would have wanted. Besides, all Rhys's friends were going to be there and I didn't want it to be too grim for them.

A few days before the funeral, we sat down with Owen to talk about who would be the four pallbearers. Obviously Ste wanted to carry Rhys and Ste's two brothers, Neil and Dave, were also going to step in but we weren't sure whether Owen would want to.

'Do you want to carry him?' I asked. 'You don't have to. It's totally your decision. You can change your mind on the day.'

In a quiet voice, but without hesitation, Owen said, 'Yeah, I'll carry him.'

On the day of the funeral, I asked him again. 'Are you OK? Do you still want to carry the coffin?'

'Yeah, I'm fine,' he said. I was so proud of him for wanting to do that for Rhys.

Barry also said, 'If you want to write any letters, or put any keepsakes in, I'll put them in the coffin for you.' So we put in his favourite football trophy, the Goal of the Season one from his Fir Tree FC game, a teddy, quite a few letters from us and other family members and photos of us all.

On the morning of the funeral, I got showered and dressed in a daze. From early on, people were arriving, flowers were arriving and the whole house was a hive of activity but I was just focusing on getting through the day. I told myself that if I could get through today, I could cry and wail and fall apart tomorrow. That's what I concentrated on.

Ste had written a poem for Rhys, which he planned to read at the funeral. As we prepared for the day ahead, he was sitting at the table, giving it one last read.

'I can't do it, Mel,' he said, 'I can't read it. Neil has said he'll read it instead.'

I knew it was the right thing to do. It was a beautiful poem, full of emotion, and there's no way he could have got all the way through without breaking down.

The nearer it got to leaving, the more my heart filled with dread for what the day held. I stood in the living room, with my hand on the coffin, talking to Rhys through the cold, blue wood and telling him this would be his last journey and that we would be going past his beloved Goodison Park. I told him we would always love him and that we would never, ever forget him, as long as we lived.

When it was time to go, my sister came up and silently put her arm round my shoulders.

'It sounds weird,' I said. 'But having had him home the last couple of days, it's like losing him all over again. I'm dreading leaving the house.'

'I know,' she said, gently. 'But we have to go.'

The funeral cortège was very long. There were eight cars, one for each family. So Debra went in one with her daughters, then Ste's brother Neil with his family and so on, and then friends and neighbours following on behind. You couldn't move in our street. The cars were parked up the road outside our house and the entire road was chock-a-block with people and cars. I was shocked to see a couple of hundred lined up outside our house.

'Look at all these people,' I said to Ste. 'Why have they all turned up here?' I still had no idea that was a mere fraction of what lay ahead for the rest of the day.

The family climbed into their cars first and the funeral directors put Rhys's coffin in the hearse. The three of us and Ste's mum Doreen were to go in the first car behind. I was really worried about Doreen. She was on her own, having lost Ste's dad, David, in May 2003 and she doted on her grandchildren. She was devastated by the loss of Rhys and every time she looked at me she would start crying or hugging me.

The journey was silent and I was just crying all the way. We were told we had to take a certain route, for logistical reasons, because of the number of people they were expecting, but we were adamant that we had to go past Goodison Park on the way. People were lining the streets outside the stadium and the pavement was piled up with floral tributes to Rhys. We stopped there briefly and then we drove down to Everton Valley and past a secondary school, Notre Dame College. The school had brought all the kids out onto the pavement and, as we passed, they stood in silence with their heads bowed.

There were hundreds of kids standing outside to pay their respects, and we were really moved by the gesture.

We were amazed by the people we saw en route and there were thousands more when we got to Liverpool Cathedral. As the car pulled into the approach to the cathedral, the funeral director, Barry, got out of the hearse to walk slowly in front. We could see all these people, lining the streets as far as the eye could see, and inside, the cathedral was packed.

'Oh my God,' I thought. 'Where have they all come from? They've all taken time out to come to Rhys's funeral.' It was surreal. But I had no words to describe my feelings at that point. All I could say was, 'Is my mascara all over my face?'

Seeing the huge crowds, I finally understood the reasoning behind the police's decision to have the funeral at Liverpool's biggest church. 'You couldn't even get all these people into the cathedral, let alone the little church we had chosen,' I thought. I was overwhelmed. I just didn't expect the outpouring of grief that we saw that day, from so many people who didn't even know Rhys. Everyone seemed genuinely upset and we saw so many people crying that day and, in a way, that was helpful to me. To know so many people cared.

At the cathedral door, Debra took my arm and led me inside as Ste, Owen, Neil and Dave prepared to carry the coffin into the cathedral. Walking down the long aisle, I could feel all eyes on me and, while I could see the huge building was packed, I was too blinded by tears to register who everyone was at first. All I could see was a sea of blue and red, with the occasional splash of other colours breaking up the blocks of football shirts.

Soon after I sat down, the *Z Cars* tune – Everton's theme – started playing and the boys began their slow walk down the aisle, with Rhys on their shoulders. The congregation broke into spontaneous applause, which sounded thunderous as it echoed around the cavernous space of the cathedral.

Standing at the front, watching Owen carrying the coffin, the tears streamed down my face. I thought, 'Oh my God, he's seventeen and he's carrying his little brother in a coffin.' It all felt so wrong. But, in that moment, I couldn't have been prouder of Owen for having the strength to do that.

Rhys's coffin looked so small. It was probably because of the vast space of the cathedral, but it just looked tiny to me and it broke my heart to think that was my boy.

After placing the coffin at the front of the cathedral, Ste and Owen came and sat either side of me, and took both my hands in theirs as Neil stood up to recite Ste's beautiful tribute to our son.

Glistening eyes and cheeky face, angel's halo out of place
You to me are my whole world, wrapped up special in one word
Into trouble into fights, into many sleepless nights
Yours is the voice I always heard, wrapped up special in one word
Many hours of giggling fun, you really are a wonder son
Flying freely as a bird, wrapped up special in one word
Wrapped up special in one word, all the special times we shared
And you are now asleep at peace, wrapped up in a word, Rhys.

After Neil sat down, nine of Rhys's friends came up to light candles at the altar. All his friends had turned up in football shirts and I know it was hard for them to go through this. They were so young.

Rhys had a really good group of lads around him and they were all close. Losing him at this point was especially tough, because they had just finished primary school and were all going to different secondary schools, so they were being split up. This was the last summer they were all spending together and it was heartbreaking for them to have him ripped away so brutally. Their mums all came round to see us, either before or after the funeral, and they all told me their boys had taken it pretty hard. That little group still go and see him all the time, especially on his birthday and at Christmas, and they leave single roses with their names on.

The Everton and Liverpool players were sitting in separate pews, in suits rather than football shirts. The whole Everton team were there including Rhys's favourites – Mikel Arteta, Tim Cahill, Andy Johnson and Joseph Yobo – and another player, Alan Stubbs, read the meditation 'Walking With Grief' during the service.

At the end of the service, the bishop read his sermon, and said he was glad to see the bright colours worn by the mourners because they reflected the 'Warmth and fun' of Rhys's life. He apologised, jokingly, for his robes being red instead of blue.

He also praised us, saying, 'Your love for Rhys, your dignity and your family life have shone out and restored hope and honour to our community shamed by such a crime,' and he called Rhys 'beacon of light for our city.' It was a lovely eulogy but I remember thinking, 'I don't want him to be a beacon of light, I want him to be home, with us, being a normal little boy.'

Looking around the cathedral, I could see a lot of familiar faces – our family and friends, Rhys's friends with their parents and Owen's friends too. Dave Kelly was there with a lot of the investigative team and the paramedics who had tried to save Rhys had showed up, and I was glad they came. But there was also a whole host of dignitaries I had never met and who had never heard of Rhys before he was murdered. I didn't know who they were and none of them spoke to me, as far as I can remember.

Owen was dumbfounded as to why all these people who didn't know Rhys, never spoke to him or saw him or knew anything about him, were at his funeral. He couldn't get his head round that. I had to tell him, 'People are just showing their support for us. Practically the whole of Liverpool is out to show how shocked they are by what happened.' If Owen had had his way the funeral would have been restricted to the immediate family and no one else, but that wasn't going to happen.

Although I was trying to justify their presence to Owen, part of me was still thinking, 'What *are* you doing here?' Don't get me wrong, Rhys would have been made up that the Everton football team were there, but then there were all these other people turning up and I couldn't see why they would want to be at my son's funeral.

After the final hymn, 'Abide With Me', the coffin was carried out of the cathedral and, as I stood up to walk behind, I felt my legs just go from under me. They felt like jelly. Debra had a hold of me round the waist and it was a good job she did or I would have ended up on the floor.

Outside the cathedral, the hearse stood with its back open, ready to take Rhys to the cemetery, where we were having a private burial with just close family. As the pallbearers slowly slid the coffin into the back I suddenly thought, 'This is the last time I am going to be this close to him. After this, that's it.' The thought was devastating. Without thinking, I bent down and kissed the coffin. It wasn't something that I thought about doing or planned in advance. I just did it because I realised that I would never be able to kiss him again. This was my last chance to kiss him goodnight, the way I had every night for the last eleven years.

The cemetery that Rhys is buried in is the other side of the city from us, which was another compromise we made after taking police advice.

'We understand what you're saying,' they told us. 'But because these gangs are all fighting over the postcode for the selling of drugs, it would be better if Rhys wasn't in this postcode. The last thing you want is for someone to vandalise that grave.'

It's difficult to believe anyone would do that but, the police assured us, that's how low some of these gang members will sink and that's why he's on the other side of the city. Ste and I have always shared a car, so I can't always drive over to the grave when I feel I want to. It breaks my heart sometimes that I can't just walk down and see him whenever I like. I often think if he was just down the road I could go along and sit and have a chat to him, but I can't.

At the cemetery, only close friends and family were allowed and this was our real chance to say goodbye. We laid flowers and said prayers around the grave and then he was lowered into the plot, and we each placed a rose onto the coffin. All of us were inconsolable with grief, and all of us were in tears as we said our goodbyes. The thought of Rhys under the cold earth was more than I could bear.

After the ceremony, Everton football club had put on a spread for us at Goodison Park. By choice, we only invited family and close friends to have a drink and a bite to eat so we could remember Rhys with people who knew and loved him.

When we got to the ground, they had set up a marquee and laid on the food, and they were handing out drinks. Ste got me half a lager and that was the first drink I'd had since the day Rhys died. I don't even think I drank it all in the end.

Throughout the whole day, Owen was amazing. He gets a lot of his strength from his dad and they are very similar in how they deal with their emotions, by keeping them close to their chests. But he was also very protective of me. At the funeral and the wake, when people came over to speak to me, he'd see when it was getting too much for me and he'd say, 'Leave my mum alone for a while.' Or he'd put his arm round me and usher me away. I was so proud of him.

When we left Goodison Park, the family went back to my sister's and that's when it all became too overwhelming for me. Having willed myself to get through the day, when I was back in the calmer surroundings of home it began to really sink in, that it was final, that he was actually gone now.

I told Ste I just wanted to go home so the three of us got a taxi and drove home in silence – no more words to say. We were all drained by the day.

# CHAPTER FOUR

# The Waiting Game

**THE PERIOD AFTER** the funeral was when I really hit rock bottom. Just like I explained to Owen when everyone had turned up on our doorstep, people have their own lives to lead and, after the funeral, they went back to them. They had to go back to work, because everyone has got bills to pay, friends and relatives who had come from other parts of the country had to go home and everything went back to normal – for everybody but us. Our world was never going to be the same again. As Ste had said in that first appeal, 'We've lost our world and the world has lost a good guy.' At that point, it really hit both me and Ste, and the grief was overwhelming. We both went through a very bad time.

Although I come from a big family – I grew up with three brothers and three sisters – I am closest to my sister Debra, both geographically and emotionally. In the weeks before and after the funeral, despite her own deep grief over the nephew she adored, Debra was brilliant with me. I know she was extremely worried about me and didn't think I would be able to deal with the loss of Rhys, but she wasn't over the top and she never crowded me. She was just around, being there for me. Even when I would say 'Don't bother coming over' or 'I'm OK', she would come anyway.

At the time, I found it hard to keep going over and over the same conversations with family and friends. The phone was constantly ringing with people asking how I was and how we were coping. But I was so emotionally exhausted, I didn't really want to keep saying the same things so I stopped answering the phone to anyone at all. I found it easier to text instead. Every time the phone rang, I'd see whose number it was and text them, 'I'm OK.' But I couldn't get away with that when it came to Debra. She'd be at the door, saying, 'You're not OK though, are you? Let me in.' Then she'd make me endless cups of tea, or cook something for us because she knew I didn't have the energy or inclination to carry on with 'normal' things like putting tea on the table every night. I couldn't see the point.

To be honest, I don't remember much about the next few months. I spent a lot of time in Rhys's room, just sitting on his bed, thinking or crying, looking at his things, or just staring into space.

At night, I'd look around at the room where he should be asleep, open his wardrobe where the school uniform that we had bought for senior school hung untouched and unworn, ready for his first day. On his desk, his pens and pencils, his new maths set lay unopened. His brand new scientific calculator was there in its pack. His smart black shoes were still in the box, shiny and unscuffed, and his new PE trainers, which would have been covered in mud in days had he made it to school, were still lying pristine in their box. Looking back at how excited he was, it was heartbreaking to think he would never wear those things to his first day at secondary, or experience the rollercoaster of nerves and excitement that a new start brings.

As I sat on the bed, I could see the pile of odd socks that had mounted up on top of the wardrobe. Every night, when he got home from school, Rhys would run upstairs to change out of his uniform and, as soon as he had taken his socks off, he would roll them up into a ball and kick them about the room like a football. With limited space, he would smash these sock-balls against the wall and they would often end up on top of the wardrobe. But Rhys was too small to fetch them down so there they stayed, until Ste or I collected them. There were always plenty of odd socks in the wash, and their opposite pairs could be lurking anywhere in the room – under the bed, behind the drawers. Just another by-product of Rhys's obsession with the beautiful game. It would be a long time before

I could bring myself to take the socks down from the top of the wardrobe.

For comfort, as I sat in Rhys's empty room, I would cuddle his pillow or his favourite cuddly toy, which still sat on his bed, as it had since he was a baby. The huge gorilla, which stood about three feet tall, had been given to Rhys by a close friend of mine when he was a baby, and it was his favourite.

Earlier in the summer, Ste and I were having a clear-out and Rhys got rid of a lot of his cuddly toys, but when we had tried to prise the gorilla away from him, he was having none of it.

'You're eleven now and going to big school,' I told him. 'Are you sure you want to hang on to this?'

But Rhys was adamant.

'I just want to keep this one, Mum,' he said. 'I've had him since I was little. I can't throw him out.' So there he was, sitting on Rhys's bed, reminding me how young Rhys really was and occasionally soaking up the tears that fell from my eyes.

I spent so many hours in that room, it got to the point where Owen started to worry about me and would come up and say, 'Mum, you need to come out of there. You can't be sitting in there the whole time.' After the first night, when we came back from the hospital, I hadn't tried to sleep in there again but I wanted to be surrounded by the memories that room brought back. To be in the place where my baby boy felt safe and happy, surrounded by love.

The house was way too quiet without Rhys running around and winding the dog up, or charging in from football and leaving a trail of mud from the front door to the living room because he hadn't taken his boots off at the door, yet again. I can't count the number of times I told him, 'Don't be taking your boots off in here!' It would drive me mad but I'd give absolutely anything to be driven mad again. In the days after he died, I remember thinking how much I'd love him to run in with muddy boots so I could say to him, 'Just leave your boots on. It really doesn't matter.'

As well as sitting on Rhys's bed, my most abiding memory of that time is sitting on the couch just waiting and waiting. I was waiting for a phone call from Dave Kelly, or waiting for one of the FLOs to call and tell me what was going on in the investigation.

In the early days, immediately after Rhys's death, we had been trying to piece together how such a terrible thing could have happened. We knew that Rhys had never been involved in anything that could have led to this, and neither had Owen. All we knew was that Rhys had been shot. The police told us that a lad in black tracksuit bottoms and hoodie had cycled up to the car park and fired some shots. One of them hit Rhys. What we didn't know and couldn't begin to understand was the ins and outs of why anyone would do this.

We had an inkling it had something to do with the teenage gangs because there had been a few instances in the area – including the murder of Liam Smith almost a year to the day before Rhys. He belonged to the Strand gang, from Norris Green, and was ambushed by twenty members of the local gang known as the Croxteth Crew or the Crocky Crew outside Altcourse Prison and shot. The feud between the Crocky Crew and the Strand – also known as Nogga Dogz – had been raging since 2004 when one of the Norris Green members, twenty-year-old Danny McDonald, had been shot dead in a pub. Since then there had been a few other people who had been shot at or murdered in gangland attacks, but we never thought it would come on to our estate. Our part of Croxteth is relatively remote as it's not a thoroughfare to anywhere and we tend not to get any problem families there.

We had lived in our close for seventeen years and we'd always been very happy there. We had certainly never worried about the safety of our boys. Both of them had grown up playing out on the close, or riding their bikes, and as long as they didn't stray too far and were home for tea, we were happy with that. The old Croxteth tends to be where the trouble is and over the years the gang violence had been escalating, but we never thought that same violence would spill over onto our estate.

In the early days we heard a lot of 'What ifs' and 'if onlys' – 'If only he'd got a lift home', etc – but we wouldn't put ourselves through that sort of speculation because Rhys was doing exactly what he should have been doing. The phrase we heard most often, and that really got to us, was, 'He was in the wrong place at the wrong time.' That upset us so much because he wasn't in the wrong place, and it wasn't the wrong time. Rhys was where he should have been. He was at football training then he was walking home, just as a lad his age should be. It was the person who shot him who shouldn't have been there, who was in the wrong place and doing the wrong thing.

Unbeknownst to us, Owen set up an account on the Everton message board to make sure everyone knew that Rhys was a completely blameless victim of a horrible crime.

In a moving post, written in the days immediately after Rhys died, he wrote: 'Please do not think my brother was part of any gang, he was just an innocent boy.

'He loved Everton, loved playing football and idolised players such as Lescott, Yobo, Arteta, AJ – to name just a few of his favourites.

'He spent all his money on every Everton kit possible just to show how proud he was to be an Evertonian. He was a cracking little player as well.

'I hope to God that the thug who fired at Rhys is caught and gets his punishment for taking such a promising life away because I do not want anybody, blue or red, feeling what myself and my family currently are. RIP my little brother, you will never be forgotten.'

We didn't know he'd written that until years later, and it broke my heart to read it. It showed just how much Owen loved his younger brother, and wanted to protect him, even after he had gone.

Although we knew it was gang-related, we didn't really know any of the circumstances and the police were only telling us what we needed to know, which is standard procedure because they didn't want us telling relatives and friends in case it somehow filtered back to anyone involved. If they got to know the way the inquiry was going they would be forewarned and might work even harder to evade justice.

After the initial meeting, we didn't see Dave every day, just the FLOs, which was understandable. He was head of the whole investigation and he had a huge job to do, so visiting us all the time would just hold him up. Whatever information was coming in, he would tell the FLOs and they would relay it to us, and there was only so much we wanted to know. Ste and I had said from the start that we didn't want to hear about every new lead and every new suspect who came to light.

'We don't want to know who it is until he's charged,' I told Dave. 'I couldn't bear to be told you know who's done it, and then for some reason you can't charge him. I can't allow myself to go through that. Until you charge him, I don't want to know his name or anything about him.'

Ste and I stuck to that for our own self-preservation. We avoided the internet and especially social media because any names that came up would have opened up a can of worms for us. Apart from the prospect of disappointment if the killer wasn't charged, we had to think about what would happen when we eventually went back to work. Although Tesco were being brilliant and not putting any pressure on us to return, we knew we would go back one day and, in the shop and on the tills, you meet a lot of people. Imagine bumping into someone who has been accused and released. I don't know how I would have handled that.

Although we tried to stay away from it we were aware, at that time, that a lot of it was speculation, with no hard evidence. A lot of names were given, rumours that friends and family had heard on social media and probably for a reason, but we didn't want to pre-empt anything. It would be counterproductive for us to start saying to Dave, 'You need to go and arrest so-and-so.' We wanted him to be able to get on with his job and the less pressure we put on him the better job he was going to do. The police are the experts so we just wanted to let them get on with it.

Within weeks of the shooting, the newspapers and media outlets were asking questions about why no one had been charged. Although I didn't know at the time, sixteen-year-old Crocky Crew member Sean Mercer had been arrested just three days after the shooting, and had been named by quite a few informants, but had been released. At the same time, his name was all over the internet and graffiti had sprung up all around Croxteth, with the message 'Sean Mercer – baby killer' sprayed in foot-high letters on walls and shop shutters. Later we heard that he had taken to travelling around in the boots of his mates' cars, he was that frightened about reprisals.

As time went on Dave was put under a lot of pressure from his seniors, including his boss, Assistant Chief Constable Patricia Gallan, to bring charges but he was adamant that he couldn't charge Mercer because he knew it wouldn't stand up in court. There was no forensic evidence linking him to the murder and no actual witnesses from the scene of the crime. The worst thing for us, and for Dave, would have been to see the case collapse.

To add to the urgency, there was the fear that the longer Mercer and his mates were free, the more likely it was that one of them might be got at themselves. As well as trying to prove their guilt, the police were keen to make sure they stayed alive. Dave wanted to see them in court, facing the rap for the terrible thing they had done, and they were no good to him dead. While we were angry enough not to care whether he lived or died, we would have felt the same had we known what the police were doing. We wanted to see Rhys's killer in court to face up to what he had done.

A few weeks into the investigation, Dave came round to see us and to explain what was going on, as he did fairly regularly throughout. He would either ring us first or the FLOs would tell us he was coming over after the breakfast meeting that his team had every morning, to catch up on where they were and plan their day around new evidence and leads.

Dave's visits were specific. He was there for a reason, to tell us something. Sometimes it was good news and sometimes just an update. Often, if he hadn't been for a while, he'd bring one of his colleagues, Mark McGuinness, Martin Leahy or Brian 'Dixie' McNeill, with him. On this occasion, over the usual cup of tea, he gave us an update on progress, although he never said he was under pressure.

'There are a lot of rumours and people are saying that we need to charge someone,' he told us. 'But I won't do that until I have an airtight case. There would be nothing worse, at this point, than to get to court and to see him get off.'

It meant we were in for a long wait before we could see justice for Rhys being done, but Dave was determined to get it right and we're eternally grateful that he did.

The day of Rhys's funeral, 6 September 2007, was at the start of the new school term and would have been his second day at Fazakerley High School. Owen, who was in the sixth form and studying for his A levels, decided to go back to school a few days after. I thought it was far too soon but he insisted.

'I need to go back,' he told us. 'I just can't sit around in this house any longer.' Ste and I were both anxious about him going back to school but he was determined. It's difficult to get inside someone else's brain and see what frame of mind they are really in, so if he thought that was best for him, we weren't going to stop him. Thankfully, Owen has got a really good set of friends. They've known each other since primary school and they're still as close today, so we knew they would be there to support him.

On the morning he went back, I forced myself to put on a brave face as I saw him off at the door with a kiss and told him he had to text me, to make sure I knew he was safe.

'I will, Mum,' he said, giving me a hug. 'But I'll be fine.'

Ste said he would drive him in to school so the pair of them left together. As soon as they'd driven out of the close, I sank back into my pit of despair, dropping the mask I had put on for Owen's sake and surrendering myself to tears. The silent, empty house just brought home the absence of my happy, noisy, boisterous little boy even more and made me feel so alone.

As well as coping with my feelings over Rhys, I was really worried about Owen going back and told Ste he should make sure he took him right to the gate. Naturally, Owen had other plans and wanted to get out of the car away from the school, and Ste let him – without telling me, of course. It wasn't until weeks later I discovered that Ste was dropping him off early, and that was only because Ste couldn't do it one day and Debra took him to school instead. She told me Owen had said his dad dropped him off round the corner and I was livid.

'I told you to drop him at the school gates,' I shouted at Ste.

'But he begged me to let him out early,' he said. 'He's a teenager and he needs to carry on as normal. He doesn't want me dropping him right at the gates. He walks in with his mates.'

Ste was right, of course, but I just wanted to wrap Owen up and keep him safe.

Paralysed as I was with despair, I couldn't understand where Owen got his strength from, just getting on with his life so soon. But we all deal with grief differently and that was his way of coping with it. For a lad of seventeen, it's a tough experience to go through. He was in his final year at school and studying for five A levels, which is difficult enough, but to lose his beloved brother, and in such terrible circumstances, was a brutal blow to him. Even so, like Ste, Owen keeps his emotions to himself. He would withdraw into his room and play on his Xbox and all we could do was ask him if he was all right and keep him fed. We didn't have many conversations where we sat him down and talked to him about what he was going through, because that's not what he would have wanted. But Owen is a level-headed boy, and he obviously decided the best way was just to get on with it.

Even today Owen rarely comes to the cemetery and we don't try to persuade him, because everyone deals with things their own way. Owen always used to say that whenever he wanted to remember Rhys he would get out one of the old Xbox games they used to play together, and play it in his memory.

After Rhys died my natural instinct was to wrap Owen in cotton wool, and it would have been easy to become overprotective. But I told myself, 'He's got to live his life. We can't let this rule the rest of his life.'

At Rhys's wake, Owen was on a table with a couple of his closest friends and they were making plans to go to Lloret de Mar, in Spain's Costa Brava, for a week's summer holiday. He called me over and told me what they had planned and asked, 'Can I go, Mum?' My first instinct was to answer with a very vehement 'No!' But I took a deep breath and somehow I stopped myself.

'Of course you can go,' I said instead. 'As long as you stay safe and phone me all the time.' I think Owen was quite surprised that I was letting him go but I knew it was the right thing to do.

Ste and I talked about it later, after I told him what Owen had said, and I told him how I felt. 'We've got to let him live his life,' I said. 'Those scumbags have already destroyed our lives. I won't let them destroy Owen's life as well. He has to enjoy his life.' Ste agreed and I think he was relieved that I could see that, despite my natural urge to protect him.

The holiday wasn't until the following summer, in a few months' time, so I had time to get used to the idea. When it did come round, Ste arranged to drop Owen off at his pal's house, as one of their parents was taking them to the airport. On the day, I fussed over him, making sure he'd packed everything he needed and, as he left, there were plenty of big hugs and 'I love you's'.

'Now promise you'll text when you get there,' I said. 'And you'll call me and text all week, won't you?'

He promised he would and I knew he'd keep his word, knowing how worried I would be. It wasn't an easy week but I knew Owen wouldn't get in any trouble, and he texted and called me just enough to stop me worrying. He had a great time and it was good for him to let off steam and enjoy his first lads' holiday, just as any teenage boy does.

Although I knew I had to give him his freedom, it was so hard for me. To start with, wherever he was, I was constantly texting him and phoning him, checking where he was and that he was safe, but I managed to cut that down as time went on. He never moaned about that. He was always really understanding, knowing what I was going through. He's always been a really good lad and he was growing up into the wonderful man he is now.

Although the police were working as hard as they could to build a case against Mercer and his fellow gang members, they were coming up against a wall of silence. With gang violence on the rise, many people were too scared to come forward and speak up about who was responsible for Rhys's murder, and others, Dave believed, were protecting them out of some warped sense of loyalty.

On 26 September, when we should have been celebrating our twentieth wedding anniversary and gearing up for Rhys's twelfth birthday the following day, the police released CCTV footage from outside the Fir Tree pub that was to be shown on the BBC's *Crimewatch*.

The grainy images of a lad on a silver BMX bike riding up to the car park had been enhanced in a bid to help identify the killer. It was almost impossible to see his face and the hope was that people who knew him would recognise a mannerism, or something about him.

We weren't shown the film before it was released on the show and I didn't really want to see it. I knew it had to be released to help catch the killer and, when we did see it, the sight of this lad casually riding around on his bike, when we knew what he was about to do, sent chills through my soul and a feeling of pure disgust rose in my gut.

As he was struggling to break through the wall of silence, Dave asked us if we would appear in an appeal, also to go out on *Crimewatch*. I really didn't want to do it, because it felt like I would be putting my crushing grief on display for the world to see and I was desperate to grieve in private. But at the same time I knew I had to do it because Dave believed it would encourage more people to come forward. So three weeks after the funeral, we were taken to the police headquarters in Liverpool, where a room had been set up with TV cameras and huge bright lights to film our plea to the people of the city to help us catch the killer.

Until that point I had never been in the media spotlight, or wanted to be, so it was all extremely nerve-wracking. We weren't allowed a script, as the producers felt it would be more emotive if I just said what I was feeling rather than reading from a piece of paper, but I had no idea what I was going to say or whether I would be able to speak at all.

Before the broadcast, Dave took us aside and told us, 'You just need to get out there and say it from the heart.' The only pointer he gave me was 'Try to mention the gunman's mother.' Dave was convinced that the parents of whoever did this were protecting them somehow. I was astounded. I couldn't comprehend how any mother could even *look* at her son, knowing what he'd done, that he'd killed a totally innocent little boy, let alone lie to save his neck. If he wouldn't hand himself in, she should hand him in. If you have any shred of decency, you have got to come to a point where you think, 'It's gone too far now,' and do the right thing. Or so I thought.

Although I knew I had to go through with the appeal, when I got out there, in front of the camera, I was a blubbering mess. My words were coming out wrong and I was crying and snotty. But somehow I managed to get out the line, 'Somebody knows who has done this. If their parents had any thought about our pain and what we've lost, they'd turn in their son. Their sister, their auntie or someone must know who it is, or suspect who it is. Please help us.'

As Dave had asked, I made a direct appeal to the killer's mother.

'She must know it is him, or she must have some suspicion,' I begged. 'Even for his own safety, she should hand him in. We can't rest or try to move on without this person being brought to justice or being caught.'

Dave also appealed to the public to study the video of the gunman in case it was a family member.

'These images may be grainy but we are sure that if this is your son, grandson, brother, friend or neighbour, you will recognise them from this footage,' he said. 'The offender and any others involved in this need to know we are determined to prosecute those responsible. We are doing everything possible to build up a strong evidential case.'

While I was wearing my heart on my sleeve, Ste was struggling to stay strong for me and Owen but he was also struggling with the way the whole thing was being dealt with in the media. Part of the difficulty for both of us was that everyone really focused on me. That's just what the media do when a high-profile case involves a child. Everyone wants to know what the mother looks like, what the mother is thinking, even when the father is there and visibly part of the family. So while everyone focused on me, Ste was left thinking, 'What about me? I'm Rhys's dad.' That's definitely not the way I wanted it but it's just the way it was and he found that difficult.

People assume that a mother's bond is stronger, because we have carried the baby and nursed them, and I have even heard people say that the mother's pain is more intense when a child dies. But the pain of losing Rhys was just the same for Ste. He loves both the boys just as much as I do but it's the mother's face that sells the newspapers, which is hard for a grieving dad to take. It's really hurtful, especially when you're trying to be strong.

That all came to a head at the appeal for *Crimewatch*. Ste said a few sentences but they didn't seem to be very interested in him. They just wanted me to speak. Looking back, there was a very good reason for that, although we didn't know it. With our appeal they very much wanted us to focus on Mercer's mother because, without her, he wouldn't be able to evade justice. Even so, I knew Ste found it hurtful and felt ignored. I could see it in his face, although he would never talk about it. The only time he ever mentioned it was on that day, after the *Crimewatch* filming, when he quietly said, 'I'm here as well.'

'Ste, it's not me,' I said. 'It's the media.'

'I know,' he said. 'It just feels like I don't count.'

He never resented me for the attention I got, but it was tough on him and I think it contributed to the problems we were beginning to have in our relationship too. We were both going through some very tough emotions and, because we are like chalk and cheese, we were handling it differently. The sadness ran so deep that, sometimes, we couldn't even express it to each other and communication was beginning to become strained at times.

The media attention also meant that I was instantly recognisable in town and everyone, with the best intentions, wanted to talk to me and offer their condolences. For a long time, I was scared to go out at all unless someone was with me, because everyone knew who I was. My picture was published in the paper, usually looking dreadful and drained or in tears. When you're consumed by an overwhelming grief, it feels very intrusive and feels like the world is watching you at your worst moment, and strangers making a beeline towards you doesn't always help.

I used to think, 'If they knew how much it took for me to get up, get ready and get out today, they wouldn't come over to me.' It took every last ounce of strength to get out that front door and face the world. I know people want to show their support, and it's great that they do, but I'm not comfortable with strangers grabbing me and wanting to hug me, and it was pretty disconcerting to begin with.

The very first time I went out with Owen, a few weeks after Rhys died, we went into town to do some shopping. As we walked through the town centre so many people came up to me to tell me how sorry they were or to pat me on the shoulder that, in the end, Owen put his arm round me and said, firmly, 'Come on Mum. We're going home. You can't be dealing with this today.' Then he marched me back to the car and said, 'Let's go home.' To be honest, it was a relief to get back in the car and head home.

Ten years on, it's just the same, and people come up to me all the time to commiserate. I'm just a bit more used to it now though and I do appreciate that people really care.

The next home game for Everton, after the Blackburn match where they had paid tribute to Rhys, was on 15 September, nine days after the funeral. It was a Premier League clash with Manchester United and initially, Ste and Owen thought about staying away but then they agreed that Rhys would have wanted them to go. He would have been excited about going to that game – even though the old Evertonian 'traitor' Rooney was kept on the bench after recovering from a broken metatarsal, so wouldn't be squaring up to his former teammates. It must have been one of the toughest things for Ste to do, to sit next to Rhys's seat through that match, but it helped that they always switched seats anyway. Rhys used to sit in between Ste and Owen because the man in front of that seat was quite short and, as a season ticket holder, he was there for every match. That meant Rhys could watch from there and see more of the game without standing up.

One the day Ste and Owen went back, Ste said that the fans were wonderful, patting him on the back as the two of them were getting into their seats. But as they were leaving the ground, Ste told me later, he went to grab Rhys's hand, the way he had at every match, to make sure they didn't get separated in the crowds. He said, 'I put my hand out to grab his and then realised he wasn't there.' It was a horrible moment for him and he felt a flood of pain after he realised what he'd done.

Later, on another visit to the ground, he was interviewed by a local reporter about his return to

Goodison Park and he explained how he had reached for Rhys that day.

'I was looking to hold his hand because there were a lot of people about and I would always hold his hand so I didn't lose him in the crowd,' he said. As a parent, he said, you try to protect your child from everything bad, and he added, 'When you're a kid there are a lot of dangers about – getting run over, coming off your bike – but being shot shouldn't be one of them.'

As the season tickets for the 2007–2008 season were already paid for, we had the seat for the whole year. Occasionally I went, but I found it a struggle to be there without Rhys because all I could think about was how he'd throw his arms up in the air or jump out of his seat in disgust every time the ref did something he didn't like, what he would have been shouting at the ref, or how jubilant and over the top he would be every time Everton scored. I remembered his beaming face after every victorious match. So, instead of me, Ste would often take his brother or another family member. There was always someone who would want to go to the match.

Even so, the following year, when it was time to renew for the 2008–2009 season, we knew the trial was coming up and I was not in good shape. The thought of me ever going to the game again was just incomprehensible. I didn't want to go back to Goodison Park without Rhys and I just couldn't take his seat. Also, with Rhys having been a junior his seat had been considerably cheaper. If we kept it for me, or other family members, it would have been expensive and there was no guarantee I would ever want to use it so it just made no sense to pay that extra money. It was hard to let it go, especially for Ste, but we talked about it and he said, 'We'll have to let Rhys's seat go then. Owen and I will just keep our seats.' There's quite a waiting list at Goodison Park, often a couple of years, so it was a difficult decision, because we wouldn't get another adult ticket easily. Remembering how delighted Rhys had been when we had first bought him one, as compensation for that missed holiday, we found it tough to let it go, but it made sense.

It's only recently, since Owen has grown up and moved out, that I have regretted that decision and started thinking, 'Why did I let that seat go?' I feel I could face going to the matches, especially now, because Owen doesn't live at home any more and I see less of him. He comes round whenever I text and say, 'Come round for your tea tomorrow,' but he has a busy life. If

I'd kept that seat, I could have gone to the match and seen him every Saturday but, at that time, I could never imagine how I would be in ten years. It was impossible to see that far ahead.

The twenty-seventh of September would have been Rhys's twelfth birthday, and that was another milestone we had to somehow get through. He had wanted a new mobile phone for his birthday. He already had a little phone but it wasn't what he really wanted and, now he was going up to 'big school', he had asked for a better one. We had looked into it but hadn't bought him one yet.

Instead of watching our excited son open his presents on the day, Ste and I went to visit him in the cemetery, where we spent a couple of hours sitting at his graveside talking to him. When Owen came home from school, the three of us had a Chinese takeaway because of Rhys's love of Chinese food, and we talked about him, amid a lot of tears.

We never go out on his birthday, because it's still too sad for us, but, every year, we mark the occasion by getting a takeaway – always with Rhys's favourite crispy duck and pancakes.

# CHAPTER FIVE

# Holding On

**BOTH STE AND** I had worked for Tesco for many years and, in fact, that was where we first met – when I was just sixteen.

I was still at the local high school and every day, almost without fail, my mum would send me out to the supermarket as soon as I got home from school. I'd just walk through the door and she'd say, 'Melanie (she was the only one allowed to call me Melanie), please can you go to the shop and get me a pint of milk?' or whatever it was she needed. So, I would trot off to Tesco in Broadway, a few minutes' walk from the house, still dressed in my lovely bottle green uniform.

Often, as I popped round the store, I used to see a very tall lad standing behind the deli counter and he always had really shiny shoes. I really like shiny shoes, so he caught my eye. I suppose I must have fancied him but I didn't think anything would come of it.

At sixteen, after doing my O levels, I decided to leave school and I wasn't sure what I wanted to do. In those days you didn't go straight on the dole, you went on the Youth Training Scheme, so that's what I did. They found me a place in Tesco, so I started there in September 1982. I was still too shy to speak to Ste and I didn't even know his name. Then came the Christmas party.

Tesco were famous for their Christmas parties, which everyone looked forward to, and I was excited to be going to it as it was my first one. That year, it happened to be fancy dress, so I went as a French maid. Ste was obviously out to make less of an impression because he went as the Hunchback of Notre Dame, but his outfit was really good fun and made me laugh. The daft costumes really helped break the ice and we finally found the courage to have a proper chat, so that's where it all started.

The following week we went on our first date to a pub in West Derby, which was actually called the West Derby but, for reasons we never knew, was locally known as the Barries. Ste was nineteen, two years older than me, but we got on like a house on fire and the date was a great success.

Five years later, in 1987, we walked down the aisle at St John's Church in Tuebrook and I couldn't have been happier. We had the full white wedding, followed by a reception at the civic centre with all our friends and family, and then spent a couple of nights at the Adelphi Hotel in the city centre, because the wedding had left us a bit too skint for a honeymoon. We moved into a small terraced house we had bought just before the wedding, in the Orrell Park district of Liverpool. Then, in December 1990, when Owen was nine months old we found a modern three-bedroomed house in a quiet close in Croxteth Park and thought this was the perfect place to start our family. We had wanted a house with a garden, and this one had a small but neat triangle of grass out the back so we loved it. Moving into our lovely new home was a really special day and it felt like everything in life was slotting into place.

By the time Rhys died, in 2007, Ste had worked for Tesco for twenty-five years, and I'd been working there for a few years too. In the devastating aftermath of the shooting, Tesco were very understanding and told us we could stay off on full pay for as long as we needed. Ste was home for three months but in the end I had a whole two years off, because I couldn't have faced going back, but they were brilliant about that. If they hadn't fully supported us, and been there to pay our wages, I don't know how we would have paid the mortgage, so we could have lost our home and everything we have. That wasn't foremost in our minds at the time but it was good that at least we didn't have to worry about money on top of everything else.

Even so, at the beginning of December 2007, Ste brought up the subject of going back to work. Tesco were putting no pressure on either of us, and I hadn't even considered it an option, but Ste had clearly been thinking about it and he was worried it would upset me.

'Mel,' he said eventually. 'How would you feel about me going back to work?'

Ste has always been on the go – he's never been one to sit around – and the silence of the house, he explained, was driving him mad.

He added: 'I just feel I need something more than looking at the four walls of the house. It's doing my head in and it's making it all harder to deal with. I need to be doing something.'

He told me he was so used to being busy that sitting round thinking all day took away all the enjoyment of not being at work. But Christmas was coming and I must admit I wasn't keen on his timing.

'Oh no, do you have to?' I said. 'It's getting close to Christmas and it will be the first Christmas without him. I need you here.'

'I understand that,' said Ste. 'I just feel that I need to get on with things and get back to a routine. Maybe after Christmas then?'

After talking it through, it was decided that Ste would go back to work in January. Because he had agreed to stay off for Christmas, I had to resign myself to the fact that he would go back to work afterwards. I didn't know how he could face it, but when it comes to grief, there's no book on how to deal with it. You just have to find your own way as to when you feel it's the right time to do things, and he needed to have something else to think about.

Although I could never forget, for a split second, what had happened, my mind sometimes played tricks on me in the early days and I would absent-mindedly act like Rhys was still here.

On one occasion, I was setting the table for tea and putting the place mats out and the knives and forks, and I automatically set it for four. I walked out into the kitchen and when I came back into the dining room, I looked at the table and thought, 'Why have I just done that?' Devastated, I sat down at the dining table and sobbed.

It was the same when I went shopping at the supermarket. I'd go round the shop loading the trolley with all Rhys's favourite yoghurts and the snacks he liked and then I wouldn't realise what I'd done until I got home and started unpacking the groceries and putting them away. Then I'd think, 'Why did I buy that? He's not here.' It was a horrible jolt and I'd soon be in tears all over again.

The first Christmas without Rhys was horrendous. Rhys had always loved Christmas and was always really excited as the big day approached each year. Like most families, we had developed our own little routines over the years. Every Christmas Eve, we would give both the boys new pyjamas and Rhys would always have a bath and then put his new PJs on and race up to bed early, full of anticipation for the next day. Owen wouldn't be far behind and then Ste and I would spend the evening wrapping their presents and putting them into two piles, then decorating them with chocolate coins and streamers. Like all couples with kids, for us Christmas was all about the boys.

When we'd finished laying everything out for them, we would sit back and enjoy a Baileys or two, looking forward to the fun and chaos of the following morning. It was a lovely time. Christmas Eve was always so full of hope and anticipation.

When the boys were younger we used to put the carrots out with the mince pie and the glass of milk and

I remember, one year, I put the Santa hat and beard on and Ste filmed me going 'Ho Ho Ho' and pretending to be Father Christmas, as if when the kids watched the video they would think it was Santa coming into the house! It wouldn't have fooled them for a second but we thought it was a bit of fun.

It had been a few years since Rhys believed in Father Christmas though. I don't remember a moment or a conversation where he questioned it, but I think when you have a brother who is five years older you probably find out, earlier than you should do, that Santa doesn't exist.

On Christmas morning, Rhys and Owen would drag us out of bed about 6 a.m., full of excitement. Ste would go downstairs and get the video camera ready to film them, then he'd wait for them to burst into the room and tear into the presents. Then he'd capture their joyful expressions for ever.

Although we had a stocking for each of the boys, we didn't put much in them. They were more of a token gesture and their actual gifts would be under the tree. Rhys's favourite presents were usually Xbox games, football strips and, naturally, absolutely anything to do with Everton. Rhys was always a bit more excited than

Owen, maybe just because the novelty wears off when you get a bit older.

After the presents were opened, Rhys would take an hour to go out and deliver presents to his friends all around the estate and then, if we were eating at ours, he and Owen would play any new games they'd got on his Xbox or have a game of football while I prepared Christmas dinner, or we all got ready to go to one of the family, if that's what we had planned. We usually took it in turns to host Christmas dinner, and we would often go to Debra's. But when it was our turn, we would have a huge number of people, with Rhys's uncles, aunts and cousins, and the house was usually so crowded we'd be tripping over each other. We all loved the whole turkey dinner with all the trimmings, and there was lots of laughter and reading out corny cracker jokes as we tucked in.

After dinner we would always clear the decks and get out the boys' pool table, which folded down for easy storage, for a family tournament in the living room. As in all sports, Rhys was not a great loser and he had been known to move the ball to a more favourable position if he found himself faced with a difficult shot. We would all rib him about being a sore loser and we'd

Even at two months old, there's a hint of that cheeky little grin and definitely a sparkle in his eye. He was a very happy baby.

Ste and Owen at home with Rhys (three months).
Owen was five when Rhys was born and he adored his little brother.

Proud big brother Owen holds Rhys
(three months) in his arms. He was
always really good with Rhys and
played with him all the time.

Rhys enjoying a day out with all of
us at Chester Zoo.

Three-year-old Rhys mucking about in the bedroom he shared with
Owen on a holiday to Gouves, Crete (1999).

Rhys as a toddler on a family
holiday in Alcúdia, Majorca.

In our back garden, when we still
had grass! Rhys's football obsession
soon wore that out.

On a beach in Majorca.
He loved playing in the sand with his bucket and spade.

Me, Rhys (aged seven) and Ste in Los Cristianos, Tenerife.

My three wonderful boys on a family holiday in Zante, Greece (2000).

Ibiza 2002. Owen had shot up and, even though he was only twelve,
he was already as tall as me.

Always the joker! Rhys couldn't resist putting on this daft wig at my 40th birthday bash (2005).

Rhys showing off his muscles on holiday in Tenerife.

Having fun on a pedalo (aged four) in Zante.

Winding his brother up in Ibiza (2002).
Those two were always playing about together.

We laughed so much at this photo.
Rhys could never keep a straight face for the camera.

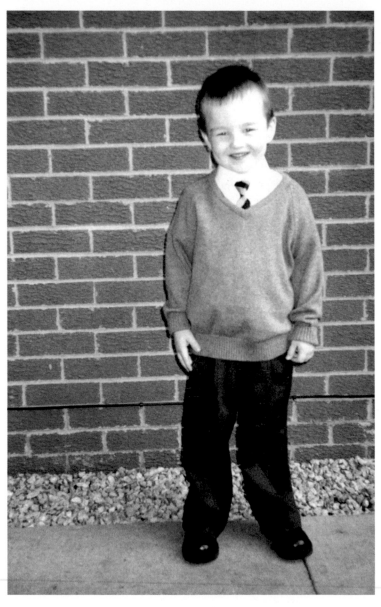

Weeks before his fifth birthday and Rhys was off to primary school.
Didn't he look smart!

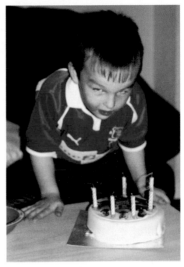

Blowing out the candles for his fifth birthday.

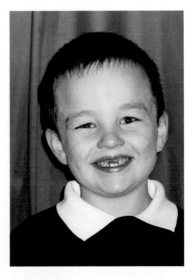

Rhys learning to ride his bike. He couldn't wait to get the stabilisers off.

Missing his front teeth in the school photo (aged seven).

The 3 foot gorilla that was Rhys's favourite cuddly toy. He wouldn't hear of throwing it out.

Our footie-mad lad was always in the garden with a ball. The lawn ended up in such a state we had to replace it with artificial turf.

Rhys gets a medal on presentation night for his first team – Witty's.

Always happiest on the pitch – Rhys playing for Witty's (2003).

Winning the trophy for the under-8s, Witty's.

Rhys always kept his kits.
We counted twenty-three when we finally cleared his room.

One of the many medals and trophies Rhys collected over the years.
This one was for a tournament in 2004.

The Rhys Jones Complex, opened by Ste and I in August 2013,
provides sporting facilities for the estate.

The plaque inside the Rhys Jones Complex.

Rhys (second on the left, back row) with the Fir Tree team.
Manager Steve Geoghegan (left) was first to Rhys after he was shot and
Tony Edge (right) came to tell me.

Ste with
Rhys's Fir Tree
teammates
on a visit to
Stormont for
a tournament.
Look how
they've grown.

To mark the tenth anniversary, we refurbished the grave and added Ste's poem.

The carving we found on the tree, two years after Rhys died.

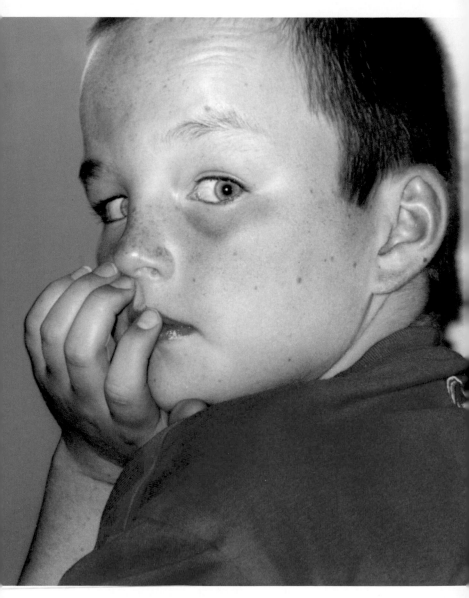

A rare, serious moment caught on camera in Gran Canaria,
a year before he died. My beautiful blue-eyed boy.

all be laughing over it, and Rhys would always end up laughing along.

After that it would be all manner of silly games for the rest of the evening. Who Am I? – when someone sticks a Post-it note with someone famous on it to your forehead and you have to guess who you are – was one of the family favourites and, as ever, Rhys was pretty competitive.

When Christmas night was over, Rhys would still be excited for the annual Boxing Day match at Goodison Park, which had a special festive atmosphere all of its own and was another highlight for the boys.

That first Christmas, I couldn't even bring myself to put up a Christmas tree without Rhys being there to help me decorate it, and I didn't put up a single scrap of decoration in the house. There was nothing to celebrate as far as I was concerned and I was dreading Christmas Day. The thought of waking up in the morning without Rhys jumping on our bed, impatient for us to get up and get downstairs, was something I couldn't even contemplate.

I don't remember doing any Christmas shopping that year. We must have bought something for Owen, but I can't remember what it was or whether I went out to buy it. In those few months after Rhys died, I never really left the house. I couldn't go out on my own because I would get accosted by people and, even if I went with Ste or Owen, I found the attention hard to handle.

In the run-up to Christmas, I told everybody we wanted to be left alone on Christmas Day and we didn't want people popping in. Even so, we were inundated with invitations from kind family and friends, saying 'Come to ours for Christmas dinner' or 'Just pop in for an hour' and 'Don't be sitting in, come to us', but I couldn't accept any of them in advance. I just didn't know what I wanted to do on Christmas Day, and how I would even get through the day at all.

Besides, while I knew people were worried about us and wanted to help, I was also aware that having us there would put a dampener on their Christmas too. It's Christmas and they all wanted to have a good time and I didn't want to be sitting there all miserable while they were trying to have fun.

In the end, the three of us agreed we would go to my brother Billy's house, just for dinner. Ste and I felt that we needed to do that much, if only for Owen's sake.

Ste said, 'We'll just go. If it's all too much we'll come home.'

On Christmas morning, Ste and I went to the grave and spent a couple of hours there, talking to Rhys, as we have done every Christmas since. Even now, I still go to the cemetery three times a week to see him, and chat to him about what's going on in our lives, about how rubbish Everton are playing at the minute, about their latest game. I usually go twice on my own during the week and the two of us will go together on Sunday. People are often surprised that ten years down the line I'm still going three times a week, but I like going and sitting there and I feel close to him when I'm there. There's a bench I can sit on but, because so many people come along and want to chat to me, I often just sit in my car. I get myself a coffee and sit in the passenger seat with the window down, so I can still talk to him.

On that Christmas Day, we talked to him about who was doing what and the Christmases we'd had together in the past, and the Boxing Day match at Goodison Park, which was Everton vs Bolton. Then we headed over to my brother's house for lunch.

When we arrived Billy and his wife Betty were there with Debra and her children. We had Christmas lunch and afterwards we took part in a quiz that Billy had put together. But we didn't stay too long and, after a few more drinks, we came home. It was just another day that we had to get through and Christmas was no fun without Rhys. The gaping hole in our lives was with us all the time but special occasions, like birthdays and Christmas, drove it home even more. Christmas was never going to be the same again.

Every day was still a huge struggle and the nights were no better. There was no release in sleep, as I barely slept at all. Although we'd go to bed almost relieved that we had made it through another day, I would lie awake for hours and, if I closed my eyes, all I could see was Rhys. Sometimes he would be at his happiest, laughing and running around, or trying to make me and Ste laugh, all the while with his mischievous little grin. Other times, on my worst nights, I would see flashbacks to that terrible day, to Rhys in that car park or lying in hospital, covered in blood.

In the morning, I'd wake up from what little sleep I'd had and within seconds the whole horrible situation would hit me again, along with waves of anger, depression and utter hopelessness. I missed Rhys so badly, so painfully, every moment of every day and there was nothing I could do about it.

The only thing that I could focus on, to give me some sort of hope, was that they would catch whoever did this and we would see justice done.

In January 2008, not long after New Year, Ste did as he had said and went back to work at Tesco. Even though he'd waited until after Christmas, I was still a bit upset and I really didn't want to be on my own, plus I worried that he had gone back too soon for his own good, but I understood he needed to occupy himself somehow.

Instead of going back to the night shift, he initially went back on days, which I was grateful for. I hated being alone in the house but I didn't want to go anywhere, so I sat on the couch, eating junk food and watching trash TV, unable to find the energy to do anything else. Debra would phone several times a day and would pop round unannounced, which helped a lot, but most days were just awful.

At least with Ste changing his hours it meant he was home at a reasonable time so we could spend the evenings together. Not that I was great company at the time and, while we were sharing in our grief, things weren't always great between us because of the overwhelming sadness we both felt and our very different ways of dealing with it.

Sometimes, when things were a bit strained between us, I remembered what one of the FLOs had said in the days after Rhys died. She sat opposite me and Ste in our living room and started talking about the stress and strain that is put on a relationship when something like this happens. Then she blurted out, 'You do realise that your marriage won't survive this, don't you?'

I was dumbfounded. I looked at her, and looked at Ste, and he subtly shook his head, as if to say, 'Don't say a word.' He could see I was incensed and I was on the verge of erupting. I wanted to shout, 'How dare you! How dare you say that!' But she hadn't finished.

To add insult to injury, she then started listing the couples who had split after the murder of a child, including parents of murdered toddler James Bulger, Sara Payne's parents and a whole long list of parents who had suffered the loss of a child in horrific circumstances. I sat there, stunned, just looking at her thinking, 'Do we really need to hear this? Why would you even say that?' How could you say to any couple their relationship won't survive, let alone a couple who were already going through the worst thing imaginable? It was a pretty crass thing to say and Ste and I had been solid for almost twenty-five years, married for twenty, so I was convinced nothing could tear us apart, even this. But looking back, as the months moved on, some cracks had begun to show.

One particular moment I can remember, before Ste went back to work, really showed how differently we were coping. I was having a really bad day and, as on all my worst days, I couldn't do anything except lie on the couch, crying. I would lie like that for hours, incapable of getting dressed, showering or even eating. I still wouldn't have the telly or radio on. I wanted no connection with the world outside our house and our own personal heartbreak.

As I lay there that day, all I could hear was Ste upstairs laughing, and I had no idea what he was laughing at. Eventually, I couldn't stand it any more so I forced myself off the couch and went up to see what he was doing. He was sitting in our bedroom, watching DVDs of all our recent holidays as a family. He was laughing and smiling. He was having a good day and I was having a bad day and that was so difficult to bear, but he was just getting through it the best way he could.

While I let my feelings pour out every day, Ste just couldn't. He locked everything away. Even though I tried to talk to Ste about his feelings, he couldn't talk about any of it to me at all. At that point, to be honest, I don't think he could even look at me because all he could see was devastation, and he was wondering if I was even going to survive it. I suppose his natural instinct as a husband and father was to make things right for me and for Owen, but he couldn't. Nobody could make this right.

Although we weren't being told much about the investigation, the police were making a lot of headway and had already arrested Sean Mercer along with his suspected accomplices Dean Kelly, James Yates, Nathan Quinn and the lad who would later be known as Boy M. After the *Crimewatch* appeal went out another twelve people from the Croxteth and Norris Green areas had come forward and named Mercer as the gunman so, while he didn't tell us, Dave was already pretty sure he had the right suspect. The problem was getting the charges to stand up in court and, in the meantime, he had no choice but to release all of the suspects on bail for the time being.

At the beginning of September, after tracing the movements of Mercer, Yates and Kelly in the hours after the shooting, they raided the lock-up of one of their friends, Melvin Coy, and found empty petrol cans, which were to prove crucial to the case later on. Then, on 30 September, there was another breakthrough when they found the gun that had been used to fire at Rhys, along with another gun and ammunition, in the loft space at the home of Boy X, as he was to be named in the trial. Days later Boy X was arrested as he came home from a holiday in Florida. He had been warned about the arrest by Mercer but his family persuaded him to cooperate with the police, and that was to prove crucial in the end.

While all this was going on, without us being given any detail, Dave Kelly was keen to let us know they were doing everything they could to get this right, even though it seemed to be dragging.

He invited us down to the incident room at Mather Avenue Police Station, a huge complex of buildings where the training facilities and the Merseyside Mounted Police were housed. We were told that they had put the incident room there because that was where Pat Gallan, the assistant chief constable, rode her horse, although I don't know if that is true.

As soon as we got there, we were led into a huge room where a large number of police officers were beavering away at their desks with their heads down.

There were stacks of papers on their desks and the walls were lined with shelving from the floor to the ceiling, and each shelf was rammed full of identical ring-binder files with the name Rhys Jones written down the spine. There must have been five or six shelves piled high with files, floor to ceiling, and there was not a gap. They were solid.

After a quick look round, Dave introduced us to a few of the officers and they showed us all the evidence they were going through and explained a bit about how they were processing the vast amounts of information they had gathered. They said each new lead triggered an action and the action was dealt with and that might bring another action. They had some sort of method whereby they went through every tiny scrap of information, until it was exhausted and there were no more answers to be had.

When we had been asked, we thought it would be a good idea to see what was going on and how they were progressing but, in truth, it turned out to be really traumatic. Although Dave had insisted his team take all the photographs of the alleged assailants down from the wall, so we couldn't see who the suspects were, as soon as I walked in all I could see were photos of Rhys everywhere and I was soon fighting back tears again. It was hard to see his cheeky face plastered all over a murder inquiry incident room and it really upset me. But it was clear everyone was working very hard, which was some comfort.

Having had no dealings with the police in the past, I found it quite informative, and I think they just wanted to show us that they were doing their best, that they were determined to get there.

Friends and family were constantly asking us if there had been any developments in the case, and I had to say, 'Honestly I don't know.' But that's exactly why Dave was keeping everything on a need-to-know basis, and was really only telling us what was also being released to the press in case we heard it elsewhere. There was a whole lot of stuff going on in the investigation that we just didn't know and, until the time was right, we didn't need to know.

Even though the wheels seemed to be moving slowly, I never doubted, for one second, that Dave would get whoever did this. There is just something about Dave that made me believe in him, absolutely. He's a genuine, down-to-earth person and a dad himself and I really felt a connection with him. I knew he would move heaven and earth to do his job and find the culprit.

In the months after the shooting, during one of his updates, he told us, 'I might be getting pressure from all sides but you are the two people I'm getting no pressure from at all.'

'You're doing your job and we know that,' I said. 'We don't want to put pressure on you, we just want you to do this for us, to do it for Owen and most of all for Rhys.'

We always had faith in Dave and his team and that kept us going through those terrible months.

Shortly after Rhys's funeral, a few people from our estate approached us because they wanted to set up a charity in Rhys's name and they wanted to use the money to build a community centre for the kids.

It was literally a couple of weeks after Rhys died and, to be perfectly honest, I didn't even realise what I was signing. Even the FLOs thought it was a little bit too soon. Personally, I agree that it may have been too early, but the idea was to strike while the iron was hot, while Rhys was still fresh in people's minds. It seemed like a good idea because the pitches that Rhys used to play on were just a field, really, and there was nothing on the estate for the kids. There was no leisure centre or sporting facilities, so we agreed to let them start the fundraising.

In my opinion, the charity had a dual purpose. As well as raising money for a good cause, and something that would benefit the whole community, people genuinely wanted to reach out to us, but really didn't know what to do. This gave them a way of showing how much they cared and, hopefully, they could take some comfort in that.

The charity was named the Rhys Jones Memorial Fund and a local man, Dave Saville, stepped up to run it. There were a lot of high-profile donations. American producer David Gest appeared on the quiz show, *Are You Smarter Than a 10-year-old?* and won £100,000, which he donated towards the fund. The community centre received some really generous anonymous donations and later, in 2010, Liverpool manager Rafa Benitez donated a very large sum, even though he had moved on to Milan, because he said that Rhys's story had affected him so deeply while he lived in the city. Touchingly, he also said he was digging deep because many people in Liverpool couldn't afford to.

In an interview with the BBC, he said: 'I am doing this on behalf of the people who cannot. I know that every person on Merseyside would have loved to give the fund a donation but they are in hard times and can't find the extra cash.

'To think that this lovely little boy was taken from his family in such awful circumstances is heartbreaking.' He also said he remembered us coming to the match at Anfield, soon after Rhys's death, and said, 'They were so dignified, it is something I will remember for a long time.'

While we were getting large donations from generous celebrities, others were doing what they could too. The girls I worked with at Tesco held a charity night at the Adelphi Hotel and raised £26,000 in one night, from ticket sales, raffles and activities, which was absolutely amazing. Lots of local businesses donated prizes and we got signed shirts and signed football boots from Liverpool and Everton to auction off, which was really good.

We both got involved in the fundraising fairly early on, going to events and helping organise a few things, and I was hoping it would help us take our minds off things. It seemed to help Ste because he likes to be busy, and throwing himself into fundraising projects as well as going back to work proved a very welcome distraction. Unfortunately, it didn't really work the same way for me. To me, it just added extra worries – what if we didn't raise enough money? What if the centre didn't get built? I just wasn't ready or capable of taking on any more burdens.

But it wasn't just our local community that was pulling together. In memory of Rhys, as the city mourned for our son, the local paper the *Liverpool Echo* launched a charity called Liverpool Unites, urging people to wear purple ribbons in Rhys's memory. We knew Ben Rossington from the *Echo*, because he did the first interview with us, and he told us that the paper wanted to set up the charity to raise funds for the community centre and also to help various other local charities, including the Alder Hey. They set the target for the centre at £100,000 and once they'd raised that, they started raising money for more charities.

The purple ribbons were to represent the city coming together as one. The idea was that the colours of the rival teams, Everton and Liverpool – the blues and the reds – mixed together to make purple, so that's the colour that was chosen as a symbol of the united city.

My brother Billy always says, 'That was down to me,' because he's a fanatical red but, on the day of Rhys's funeral, he wore two ribbons – one red and one blue. He might be right – maybe somebody picked up on that and came up with the idea of a purple ribbon.

Everton and Liverpool FC put aside their rivalry, and united to back the campaign, with high-profile players from both teams wearing the ribbons and Liverpool's then manager Rafa Benitez voicing his support.

# CHAPTER SIX

# The Silence is Broken

**FOR THE FIRST** eight months after Rhys was murdered, we had been inundated with requests from people who wanted to meet us, but we swerved most of them. There were quite a few politicians but our FLOs advised us that many of them just wanted to 'tick a box' and say they had spoken to the family, so we turned them down. We had no desire to talk to people who wanted to make political capital out of our son's death.

However, in January 2008, the then Home Secretary, Jacqui Smith, came to Liverpool to launch a policy to ban deactivated guns and we agreed to meet her in Liverpool.

To be honest, I wasn't a big fan when we met. After introducing herself, she said: 'Tell me about Rhys,' and I just burst into tears. I wasn't ready to tell a perfect stranger all about the lovely boy we'd lost and I didn't feel any connection with her. It wasn't her fault but I just wasn't sure if she was there because she was really interested, or because she felt it was the right thing to do.

After asking about Rhys she went through what happened that day and we spoke a little bit about gun crime, because of her plans to ban the deactivated guns that were flooding the streets and being put back into action. But, for us, it was still early days and we weren't really thinking about the bigger picture. We were more interested in getting the people who did this caught and locked up than getting behind any anti-gun campaigns, and that was all we could focus on.

All the requests for access to me and Ste came through the police and were filtered by the FLOs. As we got to know each other, the FLOs were able to sift the wheat from the chaff for us and would only mention the requests they thought we would be interested in or wouldn't upset us.

Even so, there were a few they told us about that were really bizarre. There was one asking if the caller could send us a painting they'd done of Rhys and there was a flurry of calls from mediums who wanted me to come for a session, which I had no interest in at all. We even got a few real cranks who would say things like, 'I can see Rhys now. He's by a river,' and one said she had seen Rhys at the end of her bed, which was absolutely crazy. I just don't believe in all that mumbo-jumbo and I wasn't having any of it.

But it wasn't only cranks who felt the need to reach out to us, and there were one or two extraordinary acts of kindness that stand out in my murky memories of those dark days.

On one occasion, there was a knock at the door and, there on the step, stood a woman with a huge lasagne in a foil dish. She told us she had lost a child and knew how it felt. Then she said, 'I hope you don't mind but I know that you won't be eating properly, because you forget to eat, so I decided to make you a lasagne.'

Obviously worried we might not feel like eating food cooked by a stranger, she then produced a series of pictures of her kitchen to show us how clean it was, in case we thought that she'd rustled it up in some greasy, dirty place. That was really thoughtful. Of course, she was absolutely right and I was barely eating at all, let alone cooking proper meals, so we did warm it up and everyone tucked in. I have no idea where she came from, or whether she was local, and we never saw her again but it was a good lasagne and we appreciated the gesture.

Another day, a lovely old man knocked on the door with a packet of teabags and a packet of Rich Tea biscuits. He said, 'I've just got my pension and I wanted to make sure you had a cup of tea and a biscuit.' How thoughtful.

Steve Geoghegan, Rhys's coach, was always keen to do something special in Rhys's memory and one day, a few months after he died, he came to Ste and said, 'I've got an idea.' Ste laughed and said, 'So what is it this time, Steve?' because Steve was always full of ideas.

'I want to put on a football tournament, for all the good kids,' he said.

Steve explained that he felt the badly behaved kids got a lot thrown at them – like Xboxes and stuff – to keep them quiet. There had been a few stories in the paper about schools offering incentives to the worst-behaved kids as a reward for improving their behaviour, but he wanted to do something for the kids from all walks of life, the ones who didn't get into trouble, and for the youth teams around Liverpool. Although we both thought it was a good idea, I left it to Ste because I didn't want to get involved. Ste and Steve liaised with Liverpool City Council and with Liverpool FC and Everton FC and they had quite a few meetings up at Anfield with Brian Hall, the former Liverpool player who had been given the position of Football in the Community Officer at the club. He was really supportive and he was a lovely guy who, sadly, passed away in 2015 after a long battle with leukaemia. A lot of people were keen to get involved, including a policeman who wasn't on our case, but who ran quite a few youth teams up in Mossley Hill, in the south of the city. He said he would bring his teams in, so they set about arranging a tournament for both boys and girls.

The first one took place in March 2008, and the big football clubs really came up trumps. Everton lent them Finch Farm, which was their training ground, for some preliminary games and more were played at Kirkby, Liverpool's training ground. For the finals, Chester City, as they were then called, lent them their home ground, the Deva Stadium.

For the motto of the tournament, Steve came up with the slogan 'Join a team not a gang,' and the police got behind the idea as well, helping out with all sorts of add-ons. The kids all got a T-shirt, a medal, a pencil case and a football boot carrier, with logos on, as well as pencils and pens. The police have funds to get these kinds of things made because it helps them to reach a wide audience of kids, so they had banners all round the pitch, displaying the anti-gangs message.

Although I didn't get involved in the organisation and fundraising, I did pop down on the day and Ste was there the whole day, presenting all the medals and the cups for the team. I was proud of him for getting so involved in a good cause, but it was hard for me to be there without Rhys.

Rhys's team Fir Tree played in a special charity shield match against a chosen opponent so that they would definitely get a game on the main pitch. It was a great day and the kids really enjoyed it although, for us, it was tinged with a large amount of sadness when we thought how much Rhys would have loved it.

That first tournament turned into an annual event with further tournaments at Walton Hall Park, which is a stone's throw from Goodison. Ste and Steve also took the tournament over to Ireland one year and to Cologne another year, pitting the Liverpool lads against the local teams, which Ste loved.

In order to fund the events, Steve set up a separate charity and, as it was non-profit, whatever was left in the pot was spent on the clubs. It would be used to buy a kit for a team or supply new footballs and other equipment, whatever was most needed, so we felt it was going to a good cause.

Steve kept the Fir Tree team going, playing in the local league, for a few years after Rhys died and all his old teammates carried on playing until they were eighteen.

As the team got older, though, Steve started to get a bit of trouble from the other teams the Fir Tree played against, both the players and the parents. One team, who didn't like being beaten, even threatened to come back and shoot the Fir Tree kids, which, in the light of Rhys's death, naturally upset Steve.

'They were about fourteen or fifteen and they ran across the pitch and hurled a volley of abuse at the parents, and threatened to come back and shoot them,' he said. 'It wasn't taken lightly, given what happened to Rhys.' By the time his own son Sean had reached eighteen, Steve had had enough.

'All the current kids are coming up to eighteen now and as they get older the arguments on the pitch get worse,' he said. 'I'm not doing it any longer.'

It was a real shame because he was really great with the kids, but at the end of the day, if he's getting abuse, it's not worth the hassle.

Sean, who Rhys used to play with and who was the first one to get to Rhys after he was shot, does some coaching now. He became a referee and he now runs his own team of eleven-year-olds, the age that Rhys was, and he enjoys it. It's often crossed my mind that, had Rhys not made it into his dream career as a professional footballer, he might have done something similar. He would always have wanted to be involved in football one way or the other, and I could imagine him being keen to help younger kids enjoy the game he loved so much.

While we waited for news from the police, Owen was coming up to his eighteenth birthday. Although he hadn't asked us for a big celebration, both Ste and I thought it would be unfair on him if we didn't throw him a party. Why should he miss out on such an important milestone in his life because of the terrible thing that had happened to his brother? None of it was his fault and Rhys would never have wanted Owen to suffer.

We decided to have the party at the house and, even though it was only March, we put up a gazebo in the garden and all his friends and his cousins came along with Ste's mum and our brothers and sisters. Owen had a great night, although I know he missed Rhys being there. It was emotional for all of us, knowing how much Rhys would have enjoyed the party, and imagining how he would have been running around with his cousins and causing chaos.

*

Over the first six months of the investigation, especially in the earliest days, we knew that the police were arresting people – mostly teenagers – but that they were all being released. We didn't know who they were but we knew there were a lot of them and by February, the count had reached twenty.

Not having any experience of these things, we initially found that frustrating and we were thinking, 'Why are they being released?' To those who are unaware of the process, it could look like the police are picking up the wrong people or, worse, the right people but with not enough evidence to convict. But over time, we began to understand the way the system works, and we realised that not everyone who is arrested is necessarily going to be charged. Sometimes they are arrested just so the police can talk to them, so they can help in the investigation. Sometimes, we discovered later, they arrest them so they can put listening devices into their houses and there are a number of other reasons they might be picked up and then released.

As we faced the six-month anniversary of Rhys's death, on 22 February 2008, we were aware of a few more breakthroughs in the police enquiry. On 20 February, after warning us first, Dave Kelly gave a statement to the press saying that they had found the murder weapon – forensic tests had linked the weapon to the shooting. Shockingly, the gun – a First World War Smith and Wesson – was among 108 guns the Merseyside Police had taken off the streets of the city during a gang crackdown in the six months since Rhys died.

Although no one had yet been charged, Dave told the press that he was happy with the way the inquiry was moving on, and said he was 'confident of a successful prosecution' of the killer.

Still feeling the pressure to press charges, he addressed the speculation about Sean Mercer, whose name was still being widely circulated around Liverpool as the prime suspect.

'I am fully aware that there has been a lot of speculation in the local community and on the internet about the name of a potential offender,' he said. 'However, we have to deal with fact and require evidence to present any case and progress it through the courts. Again, I would like to thank the public who have come forward for their continued help and support in providing statements or information.'

One thing they were yet to find was the bike that the killer had been riding at the time. With the help of testimony and CCTV footage, experts had now managed to pin down the exact make and model – a Specialized Hardrock worth around £400 – and Dave revealed that witnesses had described the bike as having a silver frame, black forks and a black seat. He appealed to members of the public to help find the bike, which he believed had been dumped an hour after the shooting.

In fact, it turned out Sean Mercer had dismantled the bike and hidden part of it under a bush near an industrial estate in Knowsley, not far from Croxteth. A man called Leslie Shimmin had found the silver frame while out on an early-evening bike ride with his young son on 23 August, the day after Rhys was shot. Recognising it as an expensive make, he had taken it home with the intention of restoring it for one of his children. After reading about Dave's appeal, however, he realised it was vital evidence and called Merseyside Police to hand it over.

As part of his alibi, Sean Mercer had told the police that another bike he had at his home, a black and orange mountain bike, was the only one he had ever used and his mother, Janette, had lied to back him up on that story. But as soon as the police had the bike frame they were able to get DNA from it and tests established a link to him. Also, it turned out he had been given the bike by an insurance company after a claim in April 2007 and, luckily, they had kept the serial number, which matched the one on the recovered bike. Another piece of the jigsaw had slotted into place.

Unbeknownst to us, the director of public prosecutions had also granted immunity from prosecution for Boy X, who had been arrested at Manchester Airport in October, and they put him and his family under a witness protection order. He was just seventeen and came from a decent family, who persuaded him to give evidence against Mercer and his mates even though he was terrified of the repercussions.

In fact, Mercer had chosen to contact him out of the blue precisely because he was the one lad he knew who had not been in trouble with the police, but that had now backfired. The silence surrounding the murder was finally broken.

Boy X told how Mercer called him twenty minutes after the shooting and asked him to get a taxi to Boy M's house, and pick up the weapon used to shoot Rhys. He then took it back to his house, where he hid it in the dog kennel before another of Mercer's mates, Dean Kelly, came round and moved it to the loft.

The director of public prosecutions ruled that Boy X's evidence was crucial to the chances of prosecution and offered him immunity, an identity change and a move away from Croxteth. It was the first time this had been granted to a youth under eighteen but it was exactly the final breakthrough that Dave Kelly and his team needed.

On 14 April, Dave rang us to tell us to expect news the following day.

'We can't tell you what is happening but there is something significant going on tomorrow,' he said. 'Please keep it quiet for now and don't go telling your family anything.' We had no idea what it was going to be but we were sure, from his tone, there would be a major breakthrough, so we waited to hear the news with a lot of anticipation.

The next day, 15 April, police swooped at dawn and arrested Sean Mercer and ten others, including James Yates, Nathan Quinn, Dean Kelly, Melvin Coy and Boy M.

That same morning, Dave paid us a visit at home and asked us to sit down. 'I've got some news,' he told us. 'We've charged him.'

'Thank God,' I said. 'Who is he?'

'His name is Sean Mercer,' said Dave.

It was honestly the first time I'd heard the name and it meant nothing to me. I felt nothing, which surprised me. Obviously I was relieved that somebody was getting charged because all I wanted was justice for Rhys. I didn't want someone to get away with it but the name was irrelevant. It was just a name.

'Haven't you heard the rumours?' Dave continued. 'There's been a load of stuff floating around social media.'

'I don't do social media,' I said, truthfully. 'I've never heard that name.'

Dave told us that Mercer had been charged with murder and that there were quite a few others who had also been taken into custody, after trying to help him cover up the crime. At that point, he didn't tell us the rest of the details about the accomplices or what they had done, but he told us he was sure that Mercer was the one who had fired the gun and that he was optimistic that he could get a conviction on the evidence they had. That was all he wanted to tell us at that point as he didn't want to prejudice the trial or risk us telling anyone crucial evidence before the court heard it.

The first time I saw Sean Mercer was just days later in April, in the magistrates' court in Liverpool. In a serious crime case, there's always a hearing at the magistrates' court first and then they refer it to the crown court for trial.

Walking into the building, I had no idea how I was going to react when I came face to face with the suspected killer of my beautiful son. But as soon as he was led into the dock, and I clapped eyes on him for the first time, my only thought was, 'Oh my God, he's so young.' He looked about twelve. He had such a little baby face. He was sixteen at the time of the shooting and seventeen by the time the hearing took place, but he certainly didn't look his age. Believe it or not, at that time I didn't feel any hatred towards him. My first thoughts were just about how young he looked and a feeling of overwhelming sadness at the thought of children killing children. What had the world come to when a lad that age can take a gun onto the street and shoot anyone, let alone an innocent eleven-year-old?

At that hearing, Mercer didn't look at us or say anything to us but the whole process was very, very quick. It took less than half an hour. He pleaded not guilty and then the judge said, 'Obviously this is a very serious crime and it has to be dealt with at the crown court.' That was it. We were in and out really quickly.

The case was then passed to the Crown Prosecution Service (CPS) and, soon afterwards, the trial date was set for October. It seemed like a really long time to wait, but at least we now had some hope of a conviction, and something we could focus on in the future.

Between the arrests and the trial, Ste carried on working but I couldn't even think of going back to work until after the trial. I was just focusing on that for six months, steeling myself for the ordeal ahead.

Shortly after the arrests, Ste and I were offered counselling. Tesco had generously paid for both of us to see a private counsellor, who we were told was 'one of the best in the country'.

But both us thought she was awful. Ste only came to the first couple of sessions and then said, 'No. I'm not interested. I can't do it,' but I persevered through a few more sessions before calling it a day.

To me, it seemed all she was interested in was the scumbags who had been arrested, what their parents did, how I would deal with them in court and what I felt about them.

'How do you feel about the boys who have been arrested?' she asked me.

'I don't really want to think about them,' I insisted.

'But how will you deal with them in court?' she asked.

She also asked me what their parents did, and how I felt about their parents, but, again, I didn't even want to think about them because I just didn't have the energy to do that. I was just trying to grieve for my son. It took all the energy I had to stand up and carry on. So I felt she was asking all the wrong questions.

As there had been so much attention on the case in the media, I confess I also got a bit suspicious of her line of questioning. I just thought, 'Why does she want to know all that? Is she going to go to the newspapers?' Obviously, her code of conduct wouldn't have allowed her to so I was probably being unfair, but I couldn't understand why she was asking those questions.

After that, Ste refused to go to any more counsellors but a friend suggested I tried a different one because, I was assured, they are not all the same. I thought I would give it another go so I found another female counsellor, who came highly recommended, but I didn't find her any more helpful than the last one. To me they all seemed to talk nonsense. This one talked about putting sand in a bottle and adding pebbles every time I thought of Rhys, or putting together a memory box. Seriously! Is that going to help me get over the loss of my son?

The last counsellor I saw asked me all about my daily routine and I told her I followed the same ritual every day and had done since the day he died, without fail.

'Every night I light four candles for Rhys – two on the fireplace in the living room and two in the dining room, next to his football trophies.'

I went on, 'I kiss his photo every night before I go to bed. I kiss him again in the morning when I get up and if it's chilly of a night, I have Rhys's blankets under my coffee table and I snuggle up under them on the couch.'

'You can't do that,' she said, abruptly. 'You have to stop doing that.' I hadn't been expecting that reaction at all and I was pretty taken aback.

'But I get comfort from that,' I said, defensively. 'Why can't I do that?'

'You have to move on,' she said.

'I'm never going to move on!' I told her. 'This is how I deal with it.'

'But you're doing it all wrong,' she said. 'Get rid of the candles and put his blanket away in the cupboard and then on his anniversary, bring the blanket out.'

Then she added, 'That's what I do with my mum's stuff.' It was all I could do to keep calm.

I am fully aware how painful it is to lose a parent – my mum and dad died within eighteen months of each other. By the time I was pregnant with Rhys my mum, Anne, had been battling cancer for ten years. Then all of a sudden, just before Rhys was born my dad, Milford, got a brain tumour and he died before my mum, when Rhys was four months old. We were all in shock, because we thought my mum would go first. Then, in 1997, when Rhys was one, my mum lost her battle as well. It was a painful time for the whole family and I miss both of them.

Like the counsellor, I have little things like a scarf of my mum's that I get out and look at, and a bottle of perfume that I sometimes have a little spritz of, because smells bring back memories. But, as I said to her, it really isn't the same with a child. As far as I was concerned, comparing the two showed a lack of understanding of what I was going through.

'I know what you're saying,' I said, as calmly as I could. 'Because that's what I do with things that belonged to my parents. I don't do it all the time, not even every year, but every now and then I'll get out a little something that belonged to my mum or my dad and look at it. But when you lose a child, it's not the same.

'I light the candles and have his blankets close because it makes me feel better,' I continued. 'It shows that I haven't forgotten and will never forget him, and that helps me, so that's why I do it.'

She looked at me a while and just said, 'No you're wrong.' I couldn't believe it. I'd heard enough. I stood up and said, 'I'm going now,' and walked out the door.

I couldn't understand how a counsellor could say that. I felt like saying, 'Would you like to swap chairs? Because I swear I could be a better counsellor than you are.'

Needless to say, I never went back after that.

Shortly after Rhys died we had been invited to meet Colin and Wendy Parry, whose son Tim was killed in the Warrington bomb in 1993. Like Rhys, Tim had been an Everton fan and he had been in the town centre buying Everton shorts when the IRA bomb went off, killing him and three-year-old Johnathan Ball. Being twelve, Tim was a similar age to Rhys when he died and, like Rhys, he had been going about his business, doing what he ought to have been doing at that age, when his life was snatched by the evil act of a cold-blooded killer.

In honour of Tim and Johnathan, Colin and Wendy built the Peace Centre in Warrington and they still run it together, so we went there to meet them. The Peace Centre is a fantastic place, a lovely building, and everything was really well organised, set out and funded. It was really impressive. Colin and Wendy are a really open, friendly couple and we warmed to them immediately. Like us they were ordinary people who found themselves in extraordinary circumstances, for the most tragic reasons, and they were the kind of people we'd have happily chatted to in the pub. They invited us in and talked to us about how losing Tim had affected them, and how devastated they were, but how something fantastic had finally come out of it.

Although it was an emotional meeting, talking to Wendy and Colin was helpful to us. At last, we could talk openly and honestly to a couple who truly understood what we were going through because they had been through it themselves. Of course, everyone around us was sympathetic and could imagine the pain we were experiencing but, in all honesty, you can never know how deep that pain is, and how physically debilitating the constant ache for your child can be, unless you have been there.

'People will say "I know how you feel" but I lost my mum and dad and I know it's not the same,' Wendy told us. 'Unless you have lost a child you don't have a clue.'

The Parrys were kind and caring and, above all, honest. They told us that we would never get over what had happened but that we would find ways to live with it. They said that their family still talk about Tim all the time and that they try to focus on the happy memories and they encouraged us to support each other, but to understand that we will handle the grief differently and we have to accept that.

As well as being concerned about how we would cope with it all, Colin asked about Owen, because, he told us, his other two children were deeply affected after Tim died. He said grieving siblings can react in all manner of ways and he warned us to keep an eye on Owen, but we never had any real cause to worry in that sense because he stayed very stable in everything that he did, and for that we are very grateful.

While news of the arrests was coming in, and Ste and I were attending the magistrates' court, Owen was beavering away and studying for five A levels –

IT, Geography, Human Biology, Media Studies and Psychology. Whenever he was at home, he spent most of his time in his room so we never really saw how hard he was working.

Even nine months after Rhys died, there were people coming and going in the house and he preferred to shut himself away, unless it was my sister or brother, or someone else he knew well, then he'd come down and chat. His friends were always there for him and they would come round to hang out, or he'd go out with them, but apart from that, he would be studying.

He must have been putting in the hours because he passed all his exams and we couldn't have been prouder. To have achieved that while grieving for his little brother was incredible and it must have been so hard for him.

On the night he got his results, we were full of congratulations for him but Owen himself was worried because he needed certain grades to get into his chosen university, Liverpool Hope, and he didn't think his results were high enough. But he got where he wanted to go. Considering what he went through it was absolutely amazing that he'd even stayed on at school at all.

For my part, I was relieved he wasn't planning to move away to study, even though I would never have stopped him. Thankfully he decided to stay at a local university, and to live at home for the first year of his degree, and I was glad I would still have him close at hand.

A week after we got Owen's results came the first anniversary of Rhys's death. It was another hard day to get through. Marking a year since that terrible event, the pain felt as raw as the day after it happened and I still missed him every minute of every day.

Ste and I spent most of the day at the cemetery, as we have done on every anniversary since. Being August, it's normally a nice sunny day so we sit there on the bench, chatting, and people are coming and going. In the morning we take some flowers and stay a while, then we go away and have lunch and come back to look at the flowers that have been left and see who has been there. The family always come, and a few of my friends and Ste's friends leave flowers and messages. Some of Rhys's old school friends, now grown men, still come by with their flowers to lay on his grave.

Even today, ten years on, the anniversary is a bleak day for all of us and there are always a lot of tears.

*

One afternoon in September, just before the trial, we got a call from Dave Kelly, saying he wanted to come over and talk to us. When he got to the house, he sat us down and explained to us that, during the trial, the prosecution intended to use CCTV footage of the moment that Rhys was shot as he walked across the car park at the Fir Tree. The video had not been shown on *Crimewatch* and was previously unreleased, and Dave suggested we should watch it in private before the trial, so that we knew what to expect and we weren't seeing it for the first time in the courtroom.

He took us to Mather Avenue Police Station, where we had been before to see the incident room, and there we were met by Detective Chief Superintendent Brian 'Dixie' McNeill and another of the chief investigating officers, Martin Leahy.

They showed us into a room where the video had been set up and then gave us a brief outline of what was in the footage.

'It is a video of Rhys walking across the car park and then falling to the floor,' said Dave. 'That's what you're going to see. It's not great quality but it is obviously traumatic.' Then we were left alone to watch it.

Nothing could have prepared us for what we were about to see. The footage was black and white and very poor quality – it was on a par with the footage of Sean Mercer riding round on his bike that had been shown on *Crimewatch* – and you couldn't see a great deal. In fact, if you didn't know it was Rhys it would have been hard to tell but there, in grainy CCTV footage, were the last moments of Rhys's life. We watched him walking across the car park, without a care in the world, then suddenly spin and drop to the floor. It was horrific and both of us were in floods of tears. It was one of the most difficult moments that we went through.

As soon as it was over, we asked Dave that the footage never be released to the press or the general public. It was bad enough that it would have to be shown in court but it was far too upsetting to be shown to anyone else. Dave promised and, thankfully, was as good as his word and it never has been released.

Helen Morris, the CPS prosecutor, understood how anxious I was in the run-up to the trial and we discussed the footage with her too. She is an absolutely lovely woman – warm, open and honest. I found her very easy to talk to, and not just about the case. We could chat about all sorts beside that.

She told us, 'If there's anything you don't want to sit through or you don't want to listen to, you don't have to. We'll give you the heads-up if there is anything traumatic coming up, or we think evidence might be difficult to hear so you are forewarned.'

We also met with Neil Flewitt QC, the prosecuting barrister, who was really helpful.

You always imagine barristers to be quite aloof but Neil was sound. He was a mine of information but also very reassuring and considerate and surprisingly funny. We bumped into him in town during the case, and he was with his wife and kids, dressed in an anorak rather than the suit or the barrister's robes, and we found out he had a real comic streak, which you might not expect from a QC.

Like Helen, Neil said he would let us know if something that might be hard for us to hear was about to be submitted, and he told us that if there was anything we wanted to know or didn't understand he would happily explain it to us.

As the trial went on, Neil was brilliant at explaining the procedures. For instance, he told us that Mercer and his cronies probably wouldn't take the stand, because they would be advised not to by their counsel, so not to expect them to be cross-examined. Details like that were helpful to know in advance.

Neil also revealed that the trial almost didn't go ahead because they couldn't get a barrister for Mercer. Not surprisingly, given the horrible nature of the crime and the strength of public feeling, especially in Liverpool, no one wanted to take on the defence brief. Luckily, at the last minute, Richard Pratt QC stepped in to do it and Neil urged us not to hold it against him, for that reason. Quite fairly, Neil said, 'That could have been me, taking that role on. We swap and change and we can't always choose which side we're on.'

In fact, we understood and we were just grateful that, thanks to him, the trial could go ahead.

'Look, at the end of the day, if he doesn't have a barrister the trial doesn't take place and we understand that,' Ste told him. 'We have no animosity towards any of the barristers. We know they are just doing a job and it is an important job, defending these people.'

Richard Pratt has got a duty of care to look after Mercer and to try to put his case across as best he could so that no one could turn round and say, 'Your barrister was rubbish because he did that or didn't do that.' They have to defend them properly so that people cannott accuse them of a miscarriage of justice, which would be a disaster. The last thing we wanted was a retrial.

In the weeks before the hearing started, I realised that my wardrobe was sadly lacking. Because I didn't work in a smart environment like an office, I had very little that was suitable for court and it was important to me that I made a good impression. I was also anxious about having my photo taken by the press, which we were told would be a necessity on the first day. So just before the trial started I went out and bought myself a whole new wardrobe of clothes. I splashed out on ten outfits, mainly shift dresses and little cardigans and a couple of suits.

Just weeks later, as soon as the trial finished, I washed them all, folded them all up and put them in the charity bag. I knew I would never wear them again. Putting any one of those outfits on would remind me of the last time I wore it, and I couldn't face that.

The girls at work had clubbed together and bought me a beautiful gold locket to put Rhys's picture in. It was a lovely thoughtful gesture and I was really moved by that. On the first morning of the trial, I slipped it on over the black suit I had chosen so I could keep him close to my heart through what I knew would be the harrowing times ahead. Then Ste and I pinned our purple ribbons on our jackets, and prepared to climb into the police car that would take us and the FLOs to Liverpool Crown Court.

Even though Dave had reassured us that everything would be fine, both Ste and I were very apprehensive at the thought of going to court, a place that was totally alien to us. On the journey to the town centre there was an eerie silence in the car, with both of us lost in thought and dreading the impending challenge facing us in the courtroom.

# CHAPTER SEVEN

# The Trial

**ALTHOUGH THE NEXT** eleven weeks were horrendous, the first day of the trial, on 9 October 2008, started on a farcical note.

As the case was so much in the spotlight, it had been arranged for us to go in the back entrance, away from the public gaze, for the duration of the trial. But on the first day, because the media always want their pound of flesh, they wanted us to go through the front so they could take all the necessary pictures and videos for the papers and news outlets. My initial reaction was, 'Why on earth do I have to do that?' It was the last thing I wanted to do when I had so many other things on my mind and I knew we were facing a difficult few weeks. But the FLOs advised us that we should do this on the first day, and then we wouldn't have to do it again for the rest of the trial, so eventually we agreed.

The arrangement was that the photographers, journalists and cameramen would gather outside the courtroom and wait for us, and the FLO, John, who was travelling in the car with us, would call ahead when we were ten minutes away. That way, they could be given enough notice so that they could get ready to film us going in and take the photos. Unfortunately, John forgot to call.

As we pulled up and got out of the car, word spread through the crowd of media waiting outside the courtroom and all hell broke loose. They all turned round, saying, 'Oh they're here!' and there was a mass scramble as they all tried to take photos and videos. Realising his mistake, John looked a bit sheepish and said, 'Oh no, I should have phoned them.'

For a split second, there was some light relief and Ste and I had something to laugh about. But it was only amusing for a minute because, when we got inside the building and walked upstairs to the room they had provided for us, John got a call from the court's media coordinator. The press had complained that they hadn't got the right shots and asked if Ste and I could come back down and walk through again.

'Can you just do this for me?' our poor FLO begged but I wasn't impressed.

'No, I won't,' I said.

'Please,' he pleaded. 'Can you just walk through again?'

'No, I'm not doing it,' I said. With all the stress I was under that day that was the last thing I wanted to do. After that, we didn't come in the front way again so, for the rest of the trial, the press had to make do with the few pictures they'd got in that scramble.

Liverpool Crown Court is housed in a modern brown building and there are several courts on each floor. Our hearing was set to take place on the third floor, in one of the biggest courts in the building, and the area outside the chamber is very open and very public. When we arrived it was milling with people, which we both found disconcerting because we didn't know who anybody was and we didn't know who was on our side, who was on their side and who the family of Sean Mercer were.

Dave met us inside with the CPS prosecutor, Helen Morris, and they explained some key points of the case. Then he tried to give us a run-down of people involved as they turned up, so he was pointing out people and saying, 'This is Yatesy's mum, that's Yatesy's dad. That's Mercer's mum,' and so it went on.

Walking into the court for the first time and sitting down was quite scary. I felt like everybody was looking at me. Even now, when I'm in a public situation, I think people just look at me and go 'Aah, poor cow,' but sitting in the court seemed to amplify that. I felt like everything I did, every motion I made, everyone was watching me.

The court was laid out so that the dock was set back and the family and friends of Mercer and the others were seated behind us, at an angle, so they were almost looking at our backs. It felt like they were glaring at us the whole time and we had to avoid turning our heads just in case they were. The problem was that we were on the front row with the FLOs and Dave Kelly while my sister Debra was sitting behind us the whole time. Every time I turned my head to speak to Debra, I felt like Mercer's mum was glaring at me.

The set-up just didn't feel right to me. Anyone who was there from their side could look straight at us and they did. I shouldn't have had to feel like that, like their families were all glaring at me, because it made me feel really uncomfortable.

But the worst thing about that day, and throughout the trial, was those scumbags in the dock. There were seven defendants – Sean Mercer, who was accused of murder, then James Yates, Dean Kelly, Nathan Quinn, Boy M, Gary Kays and Melvin Coy, who were accused of various charges including assisting an offender and, in James Yates' case, firearm offences. They all had the same short cropped hair and, apart from Mercer, who looked a lot younger than the rest, they had hard faces but it was the way they acted that stuck in the memory.

Although none of them gave evidence, except Kays, they were all in the dock every day and their behaviour was appalling. They were messing about, making paper aeroplanes, laughing and joking, turning their backs to the judge and mucking about all the way through the trial.

Sean Mercer was just as bad as his friends and seemed to be treating the whole trial as a bit of a lark. He was joking about, blowing kisses to his mum – at least when she was there. From what I can remember, she was only there three times in the whole eleven weeks.

Apparently, they have changed the courtroom since the trial and there's now a glass panel so that the people in the dock can't see their family, which is a good thing.

Looking at them and seeing their attitude made my skin crawl. They had no respect for me and Ste, for Rhys's memory, for the police or for the court. I was sitting there thinking, 'Why isn't the judge saying something to them? Why is he letting them behave like that?' I can't count the number of times I wanted to stand up and shout at them, 'Behave yourselves. You are in court.' I wanted to make eye contact with Sean Mercer and I was constantly staring at him, but he refused to look at me.

The only one of the defendants who ever looked at us or said anything to us was the lad they were calling Boy M. On the first day, when he saw me look over and knew he had caught my eye, he mouthed, 'I'm sorry.' But he was a minor player. He was only involved because Mercer and his gang went to his house after the shooting to decide what to do next, but he had learning difficulties and the bullies used to pick on him. To this day he has been the only one that showed any remorse at all.

Throughout the trial, Ste and I were apprehensive because we were desperate for the right outcome and hoping that they had got the right people, and that they were all going to get convicted and get lengthy prison sentences. But, as Dave and Helen had told us, there were no guarantees it would go our way.

On top of that, the courtroom was a completely alien environment. We didn't really know how the courts worked, as we had never been inside a criminal court in our entire lives, so it was all totally new to us, from the austere surroundings to the jargon they use. It was pretty overwhelming but the police and the CPS provided some essential support.

Helen Morris or the FLOs would talk us through what was being said in court, explaining terms such as 'arraignments' and other terms they used and translating the jargon. They also guided us through each submission, telling us what they were and what they meant. But when you're in court there's so much information going on and you can't take it all in. Sometimes when Ste and I got home of a night we would be talking about what had been said and there were parts of it I wouldn't remember at all.

One huge help to us during the trial was what they called the 'story book', which was given to us and each member of the jury by the prosecution. It was a book showing the timeline of everything that was alleged to have happened and photos of the scenes and suspects, plus reports detailing the dates and times that various events would have occurred.

It told us when cars were seen outside relevant places, when the phones were traced and where each of the suspects were at crucial times. With so much information being presented, along with false alibis and lies, the story book just made it a lot easier to understand.

As soon as proceedings got under way the prosecuting barrister, Neil Flewitt QC, laid out the police's case against Mercer in his opening speech.

'It is our contention that Sean Mercer intended to shoot someone that day,' he said. 'Tragically it was Rhys Jones who became the innocent victim of a long-running feud between rival gangs who were operating around the area of the Fir Tree public house. After he fired and missed, Mercer fired again. This time he hit Rhys, who went down in front of his eyes. Immediately after he killed Rhys, Mercer set about distancing himself from what he'd done. Assisted by others, he disposed of the gun, his clothes were destroyed and he was washed in petrol. In this way he was able to evade justice for many months, adding to the unimaginable grief suffered by Rhys's mother and father, Melanie and Stephen, and brother Owen.'

Unbelievably, the whole time this was being said, the defendants were pulling faces at each other and giggling in the dock. The only reaction was when Mercer was named as the killer and he shook his head. Even as their defence team entered a plea of 'not guilty' they were smirking. It took every ounce of my strength to stay in control.

The first few days of the trial were probably the hardest for both me and Ste, because the focus was on Rhys and the actual events of the shooting.

By far the worst thing to listen to, for me, was the report from the Home Office pathologist Dr Paul Johnson. He explained in graphic detail how Rhys was shot in the back, slightly above the left shoulder blade, and the bullet exited from the front right side of his neck. It was heartbreaking to hear my eleven-year-old son being described as 'the victim' and for his body to be discussed in forensic terms.

'The victim was 4ft 11in, the average height for his age, and well-nourished,' Dr Johnson told the court. 'There were small grazes and bruises around the knees, consistent with playing football.'

He went on to describe 'bullet wounds to the right lower neck and back' and said, 'the track passed through soft tissue and muscle, impacted the left edge of the lower neck, fractured two small protruding bones on the sixth and seventh vertebrae, continuing through the lower neck, largely destroying the windpipe.'

He said that the gunshot wound had caused the 'rupture of the blood vessels around the spinal column and disruption to the breathing mechanism.'

Hearing the pathologist on the witness stand, talking about how heavy Rhys's heart was, describing his brain and then detailing all the little bruises he had on him from playing football, I just couldn't cope. It was too much. I thought, 'I can't listen to this,' so I just got up and walked out.

As I sat outside, in bits and sobbing into a hanky, the judge's clerk came out to see me and, initially, I thought she had come to see if I was OK. Instead she said, 'You can't do that. You can't just get up and walk out.'

'I'm really sorry,' I said. 'But that's my son he's talking about in there. The one whose windpipe was ruptured, whose important blood vessels were destroyed. That's my little boy. I thought I could handle this, but obviously I couldn't.'

That same day, the prosecution showed the footage of the moment Rhys was shot, the one we had watched at Mather Avenue Police Station. This time they played it to the whole courtroom and I was grateful that it wasn't the first time we had seen it and at least we knew what was coming.

Even so, seeing that footage for the second time in the courtroom was still a terrible trauma and, not surprisingly, I started crying. I wasn't hysterically sobbing or anything, but I had a tissue and I was wiping my eyes and trying to compose myself and apparently the judge noticed. Just before it got to the part when

Rhys dropped to the ground, though, I knew I had to get out so I quietly got up and left the room.

When we broke for dinner, I saw the court clerk talking to our FLO, Jenny. Minutes later Jenny came over to me and said, 'We've had a message from the judge. He said if you are going to keep crying, he would rather you didn't come back in to court for the rest of the trial. It's unfairly influencing the jury.'

At that point, I just flipped.

'What!' I shouted. 'How can he say that the way they're carrying on. I'm Rhys's mum! Why wouldn't I be crying?'

'She can't help it if she gets upset,' said Ste. 'What about Mercer and the others messing about. Why doesn't he have a word with them?'

'I'm sorry but that's what the judge has said,' said Jenny. 'We have to respect it.'

I was furious. I felt he was adding insult to injury, letting the defendants carry on the way they did while telling me I wasn't allowed to cry. It wasn't until later in the trial that I understood why the judge hadn't cracked down on the lads' behaviour. Ste and I went for a drink with Dave and the FLOs in the little pub over the road from the court and I told Dave how upset I was at the judge's comments, and how insensitive I thought he was being.

'I can't believe the judge could speak to me like that, when they're carrying on like that in the dock,' I told him. 'I'm not allowed to show any emotion, even though I've lost my son, and yet they show total disrespect for Rhys, for us and for the court.'

'D'you know what Mel,' Dave said. 'What you've got to understand is that the judge is letting them behave like that so the jury can see it. They can see what kind of animals they are. He's giving them enough rope to hang themselves.'

'Think about it,' Dave went on. 'If you two are the models of decency and strength and he's still hard on you, while they are behaving like a bunch of chimpanzees in the zoo and he's letting the jury see what they're doing, he's letting them show themselves for what they are. Don't worry about it.'

'But it's so hard,' I said.

'Maybe you shouldn't come every day,' said Dave, but he knew I was determined to be there for every moment. If you missed a day, you would miss so much of what went on. I needed to be there every day, partly because there were so many of them in the dock. Although we knew little bits about what the charges were, I didn't know the full extent of what each of them had actually done and it would take eleven weeks for the whole truth to be told.

Even so, being there every day was torture. The boys in the dock were so disrespectful of me and Ste, like they just didn't care. If it had been explained to me, at the beginning, that this was all going to count against them in the end I would have been less upset and I wouldn't have been so outraged at the judge's comments. It was only after Dave explained it to me that I could begin to understand what the judge was doing.

In the first few days, Neil Flewitt laid out the case for the prosecution and, for me and Ste, the full story of that horrific night began to unfold.

What led up to it was the long-running feud between the Croxteth Crew and the Strand gang – or the Nogga Dogz – and a grudge against one particular Norris Green gang member, Wayne Brady. The Crocky Crew resented him because he had dated a Croxteth girl, Vicki Smart, who gave evidence at the trial. She said she was with Wayne on the night Rhys died, chatting near the Fir Tree, but Wayne took off after hearing the shots.

One of the defendants, Gary Kays, had been told that Wayne was there, on what the Crocky Crew considered their territory, and had called Mercer, who was out with Dean Kelly on their bikes. Only sixteen at the time, Mercer was desperate to prove himself to the older wing of the gang so he rode to the home of James Yates, who handed him a gun. Yates might have been the one to go himself, but he was on crutches after breaking his leg.

Mercer, with the intention of shooting Brady, then cycled to the Fir Tree and, although he didn't see his intended victim, he saw two other Nogga Dogz members on the other side of the car park.

At 7.28 p.m., he fired three shots at them. The first hit the window of the BMW parked in the car park and the second hit Rhys, but even that didn't stop him. He still fired one more, which also missed its target.

Finally realising what he had done, Mercer sped away so fast a motorist had to swerve to avoid him. He went straight to the home of Boy M, where he summoned his mates and they set about trying to cover his tracks.

First he rang Boy X, the lad who had stayed out of trouble and was scared of Mercer, and asked him to come and pick up the weapon from Boy M's house. Boy X was handed the gun in a white carrier bag and took it back to his family's home. Initially, he hid it in the dog kennel until Dean Kelly came round, five days later, and told him to move it somewhere safer. They put it in the loft.

After that, Mercer and his gang started to think about the other evidence, including his £400 bike, his hoodie, trainers and tracksuit trousers. He got a friend to bring him some new clothes and, around 8 p.m., he was picked up in a khaki-coloured people carrier by older gang members Melvin Coy and Gary Kays, and driven to a lock-up garage that Coy had the keys to, in nearby Kirkby.

There, they burned Mercer's clothes and doused him in petrol to get rid of any gunshot residue. Apparently they'd seen this done on *CSI*, which was laughable because, as Dave told us later, washing with water would have been just as effective and the petrol can ended up as evidence in the trial.

While they were destroying the clothes and any residue, another lad took the bike from Boy M's house and took it back to Mercer's, where he dismantled it, leaving the frame in Knowsley, where it was later found.

Just after nine o'clock, around the time that doctors were giving up the fight to save our innocent son in the trauma room at Alder Hey, Mercer went home.

Although Dave was convinced of Mercer's guilt, Helen had warned us that the burden of proof lay with the prosecution and the jury had to be 100 per cent sure for a conviction. Because of that, she said, we had to be prepared for every eventuality, even for them getting off. As a result, listening to the many weeks of evidence often felt like a rollercoaster ride. We would think it was all going our way one minute, only to have our hopes dashed by the next twist in the tale.

Mercer's alibi had been that he had spent the whole evening round at Dean Kelly's house, watching a 50 Cent DVD, but when Kelly's mum took the stand, she told a different story. She said Mercer had come round while she was watching *Emmerdale* – which meant it was before 7.30 – and that they went out shortly afterwards. She said Dean still wasn't home when she went to bed at midnight.

But during cross-examination by the defending barrister, she admitted she had a drink problem and was 'drinking every night and day.'

The defending barrister, Richard Pratt, asked her: 'It is Sean's contention that he was at your house between six and nine that evening so could not have been at the Fir Tree car park at seven-thirty when Rhys Jones was shot. Can you be sure what time he arrived and left?'

'Not 100 per cent sure,' she admitted.

Another key moment came when the weapons expert, Angela Shaw, took the stand. She told the court that they had found two types of gun residue at the scene – the first was found on shattered glass from the BMW that the first bullet went through, and the second was found on Rhys's England shirt. But she said that swabs taken from the barrel and cartridge of the Smith and Wesson gun found in the loft contained only type two residue.

She said that, if the gun had been the one used at the scene, 'The expectation would be that both type one and type two would be found.'

'Is one possibility that the police could have got the wrong gun?' asked Neil.

'That could be a possibility,' she replied. She did go on to say that, if the gun had been fired between 22 August and the day the police recovered it, 30 September, that would explain the absence of type one residue but when the defence barrister questioned her, everything got a lot worse.

'If the revolver was not fired after this incident and was found in the same condition as it was on 22 August, in your professional opinion, although not impossible, it is unlikely it was the weapon that was used to kill Rhys Jones?'

'It is not impossible given the possibility there are some other explanations,' she replied. 'I would say it is still possible this was the gun.'

The defence barrister asked her, 'But it is unlikely this was the weapon used to kill Rhys Jones?'

'Precluding all other possibilities, then yes,' she said.

To be honest, it all turned so quickly I hadn't fully taken in what she was saying, but Dave was worried that her evidence would count against us. If the jury couldn't be sure that the police had the right murder weapon, it would be a lot harder to get a conviction.

After the first day, and the missed press call, we were brought into the court through the back entrance, on the Dock Road side of the building. We would be driven into an underground car park and then taken in the lift up to our floor. On each storey, there were three sides – a restricted area at the back where there is a room for the jury and access to the judge's chambers, then the courtroom itself and the public area. The judge and jury area is out of bounds to the general public, to ensure that nobody can get at them and threaten or bribe them. The lift from the car park brought us out into this area, where we were given one of the unused jury rooms as a base, and we would be ferried in and out from there so we didn't have to go into the public area. But sometimes when it went into recess, or the barristers needed to talk to the judge, we would get pushed out into the public area. When that happened, we could go and sit in one of the little rooms off the main lobby that are kept for the police and the barristers.

The public area had chairs for the general public, including the families of the accused, and the press had a separate room. A lot of the reporters had seats in the courtroom but there were more in the press room, where the proceedings were relayed to them, because they couldn't fit them all in.

On one occasion, when there was a recess and we had been sent into the public area, Ste went to the toilet and came face to face with Sean Mercer's dad. He looked Ste straight in the eye and said, 'What are we doing here, eh?' It was as if he was saying, 'My boy's innocent so why are we here at all?' Ste had the strength to stay silent and in control, and he just walked away, but we were both upset by that.

The part that Mercer's mother and Yates' parents played in the whole thing was disgusting. Sean's mum Janette lied in statement after statement to the police and James

Yates' parents went to desperate lengths to cover his tracks where the gun was concerned. Although the police knew from the start that they were actively protecting their sons, we had no idea that any of that was going on until we went to court. After hearing what they had done, Dave's insistence that I appealed to the gunman's mother when we filmed the *Crimewatch* appeal, suddenly made perfect sense. Obviously he had known more than he was letting on, but at the time I hadn't realised what was going on. It was only afterwards, when we'd been in court, I understood the involvement that Mercer's mother had in covering up the whole episode.

'Oh my God, what mother would do that?' I said to Ste. 'How could you protect your son if he had killed a child?'

Yates' parents – Francis and Marie – were even worse, in my book. They had known their son had supplied the gun that killed Rhys and they tried to cover it up. They burned a sim card from inside Yates' phone so that the police wouldn't be able to prove he was a gang member but that backfired on them in a big way.

In the days following the shooting, the police had managed to put a probe in their home and the recordings, played in court, were pretty incriminating. In one, Marie and Francis were heard bickering as they burned the chip, with Francis complaining, 'It stinks,' and telling her to turn it round, saying, 'It's the gold thing on the chip you want to burn.'

Marie replies, 'That's the thing burning, the f***ing chip.'

A second recording had Yates talking to his dad, Francis, saying, 'There's only one lad who's the gunman, so there's one lad going to get the blame.'

'Do you think Sean's going to sit there and say James Yates gave him the ...?' Although the word at the end of the sentence was muffled, the expert called in to analyse it concluded he 'could not exclude' it being the word 'gun'. Yates went on to say he 'bought that three years ago' and he asked, 'What can they prove? Nothing. Can they, Dad?'

Hearing the tapes, and learning what Yates' parents and Mercer's mum had done, I was fuming. But Dave calmed me down when he told me they had been placed on a separate charge of perverting the course of justice.

'When this is over I'm going to have Mercer's mum for lying about his bike,' he said. 'And I'll put Yates' parents on trial for destroying the chip from his mobile as well. They won't get away with it.'

On day one of the trial, when we had arrived at court and walked through the public area, one of the first people pointed out to us was Boy M's mum, and she was wearing a purple ribbon, the symbol of Liverpool Unites. We knew her son was one of the lads in the dock, charged with perverting the course of justice, so I instantly saw red.

'How dare she? How dare she wear that ribbon?' I hissed at Ste. 'Who the hell does she think she is? That's not going to make anything better.' I was livid.

At that point, we hadn't heard the story and we didn't know where she slotted into the whole thing but we assumed she was one of 'them'. When we sat down, however, Dave and Helen explained that she had initially given a statement saying that Mercer had turned up at her house, that Wednesday night, immediately after the shooting and gone upstairs to see her son before the others also piled in. She also said they had then been picked up just after 8 p.m. However, she had later changed her statement to say she wasn't sure it was the Wednesday, the 22nd, and it could have been Tuesday.

Dave was convinced that she had been intimidated into changing her story and he explained that, until she took the stand, they had no way of knowing which way her crucial evidence was going to go.

A couple of weeks into the trial, Boy M's mum was finally called to testify. When she got up in court and spoke, I could hear how genuinely upset she was and how determined she was not to let these lads bully her, or bully her son, and my opinion changed completely.

Her son, who has learning difficulties, refused to come to court that day because he said if she got upset he wouldn't be able to handle it. It turned out that he had become a recluse after an incident in 2006 when, wrongly arrested for a gun incident, he had told the police who the real culprits were. As a result, he was labelled a 'grass' and badly beaten up by a group of lads wearing balaclavas and, after that, he hadn't left the house, even to go to school. I could see his mum had had a really tough time.

She told the court her son 'hadn't seen Sean for over a year before that little boy got shot.'

In her testimony, she said that she was in the bath when she heard her mum open the door and Sean Mercer greet her, before going up the stairs to Boy M's room. It was shortly after half past seven. She said that twenty-five minutes later James Yates and Nathan Quinn turned up, and she saw them come up the path because she was out of the bath and drying her hair in her bedroom. About twenty minutes later, she remembered, they all left except for her son and they got in a people carrier parked outside and drove off.

Crucially, the barrister asked if that was on the Wednesday, and we all held our breath for a second.

'Yes,' she answered. 'I remember it because it was my day off and there was an England game in the evening.'

He then confronted her with the fact that she had changed the date in the second statement, to Tuesday the 21st. She admitted she had been under a 'lot of pressure' to say she had got the date wrong.

In a new statement submitted to the court shortly before she took the stand, the jury heard, Boy M's mum had admitted her lie.

'It wasn't a mistake. It was just wrong,' she said. 'It was a lie, that's the only thing I lied about. At the end of the day, I've got nothing to lie about. My son's here. If they hadn't come to my house, I wouldn't be here.'

It turned out that their house had also been probed and, in a recording played in court, a boy and a woman, identified by Boy M's defence lawyer as Nathan Quinn and his mum Marie Thompson, were heard trying to persuade her to change her story.

The woman is heard telling her, 'You're going to have to live with this. I think you've got the days mixed up – just say you got the days mixed up.'

'I'm not telling lies,' replies Boy M's mum. 'If Mercer's got nothing to hide, it doesn't matter if I tell them he was here.'

'I think you had better think again,' says the woman.

The boy is then heard telling her to say she got the days mixed up and she tells him she won't lie.

Then her own son, Boy M, is heard asking, 'What's wrong with you?'

She replies, 'A f***ing murder!'

To be fair to her, she was in an impossible situation, and none of it was of her making. The lads just turned up at her house and her son let them in, because that was the way he was. He actually didn't do anything himself except not tell the truth afterwards.

Her own mum, Boy M's grandmother, also stood up and backed up the story, describing the events of the night and the people carrier that collected them from the house. She told the court that Mercer had said, 'I've shot someone,' after she opened the door to him.

After the testimony of Boy M's mum, I thought, 'I got you totally wrong.' I really take my hat off to her.

It took a lot of courage to do what she and her mum did, bearing in mind they lived right at the heart of the area where all these gang members and their families lived. I have to admit I don't know if I would have that courage if I had to stand up to a gang like that, but I hope I would.

It wasn't fully recognised until after the trial how brave she had been, in the face of all the pressure she was under to lie. She wasn't getting anything out of it, not even police protection, so she must have been terrified, but she and her mum were prepared to get in the dock and say it like it was and that takes a lot of guts. I believe they moved away after the trial, but I will be forever grateful that she had the courage to tell the truth.

Things had been looking shaky before the testimony of Boy M's mum but after she had given evidence, the tide began to turn and Dave said he was feeling more optimistic about getting a conviction. The following day came another crucial building block in the case, when Boy X told his side of the story. Because he was under witness protection, and had already been moved out of the area, he gave his evidence through a video link to the courtroom from a secret location. Although he wasn't in the room, he seemed really nervous and uncomfortable as he gave his evidence.

Boy X was seventeen and said he only knew Sean Mercer vaguely, from 'When we were kids.'

On the night of 22 August, he said, he got a call from Sean that he said was 'out of the blue.' He didn't even recognise the number, but he picked up anyway and Sean told him to come by taxi to Boy M's house.

Asked why he went, he replied, 'Because being contacted by him scared me. If I refused I would have expected me and my family to come to serious harm.'

He revealed he went upstairs at the house, leaving the taxi waiting, and Sean Mercer handed him a carrier bag and told him to hide it. He told the court that he could feel it was a gun.

'He (Mercer) said, "Here you are, take that. You've got to put that in yours." I was terrified,' he told the court. 'He said, "Don't say anything to anyone".'

'I took it home and hid it in the dog kennel and later Dean Kelly came round and took it out and hid it in the loft.'

Boy X also identified Sean Mercer's silver Hardrock bike as the one that was found, dismantled, in Knowsley. Even though he was on a video link, he still looked scared. It must have been tough for him to give evidence.

In their cross-examination, the defence team tried to suggest that Boy X was himself a Crocky Crew gang member, and they produced some images that had been downloaded onto his laptop. One had the words 'Fuck the Police' and another, even more incriminating one, had a picture of a hand holding a gun, with the words, 'Do something for the community – shoot a Nogga Dog.'

The defence barrister also said there were conversations on his Windows Messenger account about 'getting rid of guns' and 'doing people'.

'Loads of people had access to my computer,' Boy X said in his defence. 'I had no knowledge of those conversations.' But he admitted to downloading the images, saying, 'I clicked on it and when you click on it you save it.' Asked why he would do that, he said, 'I suppose I thought I was a big something.'

The defence barrister also claimed that fingerprints from his brother were found on the gun in the loft, and another gun that was found with it, which looked like it could go against us. While the questioning was going on, Ste was shooting me worried looks and, as soon as we got a break, we went back to the jury room with Dave and Helen, and Ste told us what was on his mind.

'What do you think of this kid?' he said.

'I suppose he's brave for coming forward,' I replied.

'I don't know,' said Ste. 'All we're saying to the jury is "believe this one and don't believe all the others." To me there's not much between them.'

When it came to Mercer's mates, particularly Dean Kelly, it was largely down to Boy X's word against his, and Ste told Dave that was making him uncomfortable.

'I don't think he was as squeaky clean as he came across,' Ste said. 'He could be lying to save his own skin. Why would they believe him and not Kelly?'

But Dave was convinced his version of events was as close as we were going to get to the truth.

'It's close enough to get a conviction, hopefully,' he said. 'And that's what we need to be.'

Whatever Boy X had done on the night of Rhys's murder, though, he didn't have the track record of trouble that the others had to their name. But at the time we, and the jury, were in the dark about their previous run-ins with the police, so we just had to pray the jury believed what he was telling them.

Many of the details of the trial were confusing, and that's where the story book came in handy. For example, a lot of the investigation had focused on tracking the gang's phone calls. Modern technology means that every time anyone makes a call on a mobile, their whereabouts are traceable. While Mercer and his accomplices were disposing of Mercer's clothes, dousing him in petrol and getting rid of the gun, they were constantly on their phones so the police could trace their positions and prove they were in that vicinity. Putting them in that place at that time was a huge help to the investigation but without the story book that would have been very hard to follow.

Although the immediate families and friends of the accused had maintained a wall of silence in the aftermath of Rhys's death, Dave said around 190 other witnesses did eventually come forward. Their evidence about the night helped the police build a picture of what happened – even the tiniest detail, which may seem insignificant at the time, can help in building a case.

For example, Gary Kays had a Jack Russell and he used to take it with him in the car, wherever he went. When Melvin Coy picked him up and went to Boy M's house that night, he had the Jack Russell with him and it was sitting with its front paws on the dashboard. Boy M's grandmother looked out the window and saw the Jack Russell on the dashboard and she told the police. One of the lads who lived in Kays' close said he saw Kays' dad looking for his dog, because it had gone missing, and it was a Jack Russell. He later retracted that because he knew that he had stitched them up and Kays senior said, 'I wasn't looking for my dog.' But once they've given the initial statement to the police, no matter how innocuous the details seem, it's there and it's recorded – even if they have put their foot in it and they don't know it.

It's amazing how the police pick up on tiny details and inconsistencies. Another example cropped up in the interview Gary Kays gave to the police. Boy M lived in a place called Delabole Road, which is a road that also turns into a close, so it's a dead end. When Kays was giving a statement he said, 'I've never been in that close.' The police said, 'How do you know it's a close? It's called Delabole Road.' Small slip-ups like that can really catch people out.

Some days in that courtroom seemed to go on for ever. Sometimes you would look at your watch and think,

'Oh God, have we only been in here for two hours?' Oddly, even though we were so emotionally involved in the trial, some of it was pretty tedious. There were also frustrating moments, such as when the defending solicitor would stand up and say, 'He's a good lad,' or 'He hasn't done this' or 'This is the first time he's been in trouble.' We knew, from talking to Dave, they were not the good lads the solicitor was trying to paint them as and most of them had form, especially Mercer, although we weren't to find out the extent of their previous misdemeanours until later.

As well as helping police out with the details of the night, the many witnesses who came forward helped the police build a 3,000-page dossier of 'bad character' evidence, proving that the seven accused were all gang members and frequently caused trouble in their neighbourhood.

I know they were only doing their jobs but every time the defence team tried to paint them as nothing more than lovable rogues, I wanted to get up and swear at them.

Throughout the trial, though, Ste stayed composed and strong and, when I couldn't watch the video of Rhys's last moments, or listen to the pathologist's report, Ste really concentrated and betrayed no emotion whatsoever. He has a very practical brain and he likes to focus on the facts. He even took a little notebook into court and he would be writing notes down because it gave him something to focus on. Sometimes, after the day was over, he would try to go over the facts with me and I would say, 'I'm not interested. I don't want to hear it. I've already heard it in court.'

Ste and I are very different in this respect. While I let my emotions get the better of me, he stays on an even keel. As Jeff Pope, the writer of *Little Boy Blue*, later said, he is 'the water to my fire,' and that's why our relationship works. But because of that, he found staying calm in the courtroom easier than I did. My sister can always tell when I'm getting wound up and there were quite a few times when, after she heard something she knew would make my blood boil, I would feel her hand on my shoulder from behind as if to say, 'Calm down Mel.'

Even though we reacted differently, the trial was absolutely exhausting for both me and Ste. We were picked up at 8.30 every morning and we'd get back home at 5 p.m., and the hours in between were emotionally draining. In the evening, we often didn't have anything to eat because we were so tired, or there were so many things we wanted to discuss about the day, and then I'd be getting myself ready for the next day. We had to just keep focusing on tomorrow and what would happen then.

Even after two months of gruelling daily evidence, the boys' behaviour in the dock never improved. They were acting like animals. I took it personally because I felt they were being disrespectful to Rhys. They were carrying on as if my son didn't matter and I was left thinking, 'You're not in the dock because you've robbed a packet of crisps. You're in the dock because you've murdered my son.' I really wanted to stand up and scream at them but they knew what they'd done and they didn't care. To them he was just a kid. I honestly believe they thought they were going to get away with it, which was the worst scenario as far as we were concerned.

As the trial went on and the evidence stacked up against them, I was still too scared to tell myself that they were going to get convicted. I didn't want to let myself believe that because, if they weren't found guilty, where would I be then?

Dave Kelly, however, was now convinced it was going in our favour.

'They're going down, without a doubt,' he told us. 'The proof is all there.' But I wouldn't allow myself to think like that. I just kept thinking 'What if they got off on a technicality? What if the defence pulls in someone who twists the story again?' You just don't know what's going to happen the next day and I didn't know how I would cope if the case collapsed.

Listening to the closing speech from Richard Pratt QC, more doubts flooded into my mind. He argued that Mercer was innocent of the crime, and that prosecutors could not prove his involvement beyond reasonable doubt, mainly because of the evidence of weapons expert Angela Shaw. He said that Mercer had refused to take the witness stand, 'as is his right', because he felt there was 'no case to answer.'

'Sean Mercer was not the gunman and the prosecution have manifestly failed to prove that [he was],' he told the jurors. 'We say, it is entirely likely they have got the wrong gunman.

'Even if that is just a maybe, even if it is more than just a possibility then there is only one verdict you can return.'

He told the court that the 'problem child' in the case was the .455 Smith and Wesson revolver and the evidence about the 'little particles' that Ms Shaw had examined.

'These little particles delivered a crippling blow to the prosecution case,' he said. 'If they have the wrong gun, chances are, we submit, they have got the wrong gunman also. We suggest that on the totality of the evidence, you should not convict.'

He also warned them to be 'dispassionate' about the case and not to be swayed by sympathy for us, or any sense of outrage over Rhys's death.

Listening to his speech was really difficult for me, because he sounded so eloquent and convincing that I was afraid the jury would be persuaded to let Mercer go.

Yates' lawyer claimed that Boy X was the person who had provided the gun, citing the slogans and messages on his computer as proof of his interest in 'gang warfare and guns.'

Being sixteen and suffering from learning difficulties, Boy M also had his own lawyer, Tim Clark, who tried to say he was 'under duress' when he helped Mercer. The judge threw that out and Mr Clark was forced to tell the jury that if they convicted Mercer, Boy M would also have to be found guilty. He went on to refer to the boy as 'damaged and horrible' and pointed out that he was 'not on trial for being horrible.' He even told them, 'The death of Rhys Jones caused a city to go into mourning. Sadly, the passing of (Boy M) would not impact on many, other than his own immediate family.' He did, however, praise the boy's mum and grandmother for telling the truth in court.

After eleven long, emotionally exhausting weeks, the trial was finally coming to an end but even then, we were in for an agonising wait.

The judge, Mr Justice Irwin, began summing up the case on Thursday 4 December, and was due to continue the next day. But several jury members were taken ill overnight and his summing-up had to be delayed until the following Wednesday, meaning a long and painful six-day wait for us. When we finally reconvened for his speech, the judge told the jurors, seven women and five men, to consider Boy X's evidence 'very carefully.'

'Please concentrate on the credibility and evidence of Boy X,' he said. 'You might on one view reach the conclusion he was more implicated with gang members than he has said. You may believe he was worthy and deserving of being prosecuted rather than being given immunity.'

My heart was in my mouth at this stage – was he telling them to return a 'not guilty' verdict?

But then he added, 'That is not the point. It would be wrong to skew your view if you think he got off lightly. That is not the point.'

He also reminded them of the phone records from 30 September, when the gun was discovered in the loft while Boy X was in Florida on holiday with his sister. They showed that, within eight minutes of the police raid, Mercer rang him thirteen times in fifteen minutes, 'an intensive effort, you may think, to contact him in America.'

He said the evidence from Boy X formed the basis of the crown's argument but he also pointed out that the defence teams had argued that Boy X had time to come up with his story while on his way back from Florida, knowing the police had caught up with him.

'There is a price for him in all of this,' he went on. 'Although he has been granted immunity from prosecution, he cannot return to Croxteth and has had to relocate elsewhere.

'Take it all together, look carefully, very carefully at the credibility of Boy X, but when you do, remember that the conclusion is, is he telling the truth when he describes the events that evening?'

He also returned to the confusing evidence of Angela Shaw, around the gun residue type being different on Rhys's shirt from that which was on the BMW glass.

'In the end, she [Ms Shaw] came back to the formula she had essentially begun with – it is unlikely but not impossible on her evidence that this was the gun that fired those three shots,' he said. 'If the link between this weapon and the shooting was looked at in terms of firearms discharge on its own, you could not be sure it was the murder weapon. If that was all you had to base your decision on, you could not be sure.

'But the crown says other evidence taken together can make you sure.

'Does the other evidence in the case make you sure it was the murder weapon? On the facts of this case, if you are not sure it was the murder weapon, you cannot be sure Sean Mercer committed the murder.'

It's the judge's job to be impartial and fair but his summing-up left me riddled with anxiety. If he was telling the jury that the murder weapon might not be the gun that was found, they might just believe that Mercer wasn't the one who pulled the trigger.

With the speeches over, the jury was asked to retire and consider their verdicts and it would be another four days before we heard what they had decided. Would we finally get justice for Rhys?

# CHAPTER EIGHT

# Justice for Rhys

**THE FOUR DAYS** of jury deliberation were torture for us. We had no idea when they were coming back in, and we were told we would only be given a half-hour heads-up when they were ready, so we still had to be in court every day. We couldn't risk going home because they wouldn't have held up the verdicts for us, and we might have missed them. So we spent many a long hour sitting around in the jury room we had been occupying over the weeks of the trial. We tried to watch a few DVDs to take our minds off the impending verdict, and we read the papers, but it was just a waiting game and it was hard to think about anything else.

Occasionally, when we knew the jury had taken a lunch break, we left to stretch our legs and have a wander around but we were afraid to go too far just in case.

The longer the deliberation went on, the more concerned we were getting as to what the outcome was going to be. We worried that they were divided on Mercer and, at that point, we weren't totally confident we would get the result we wanted.

'What's taking so long?' I asked Helen and Dave, after two or three days.

'This is pretty normal, especially in such a serious and complex case, with so many defendants,' Helen reassured us. 'It doesn't mean it's not going our way.'

Helen had initially suggested that Mercer might try to get off on the lesser charge of manslaughter, but Neil assured us that couldn't happen, given the evidence we'd heard in court.

'He can't go in for manslaughter because he went out with the intention of killing someone and he killed someone,' he told us. 'It doesn't matter who he killed, because he clearly intended to kill.'

'How long do you think Mercer will get, if he's found guilty?' I asked Helen.

'Probably around fifteen or sixteen years, I would imagine,' she said.

That didn't seem nearly long enough, considering Rhys was robbed of his entire life and our own lives had been left in tatters, but at that point, the 'guilty' verdict was the only thing that mattered.

Ste and I were asked to submit a victim impact statement for the judge's consideration. Together we wrote down the devastating impact that losing Rhys had on the pair of us, and on Owen, and how we felt the heart of our family had been ripped out. We also pointed out that that the devastation wasn't limited to the three of us but had deeply affected the wider family, and every person who knew our happy, cheeky, lovable son, including Rhys's many friends who were traumatised by his death.

We ended by telling the judge that our grief had been made even more unbearable by how callously all the people involved had behaved in the months after the event, refusing to come forward and do the right thing and, as a result, prolonging the agony of us not knowing who had killed our beloved boy.

As we had poured out hearts out in the statement, we asked that it be kept private and not read out in the court. Enough of our grief had been made public and we didn't want to put any more of it on show, especially in front of the disrespectful bunch in the dock and the heartless families who had tried to protect them.

Finally, after four days of waiting on tenterhooks, Ste and I filed into court and sat in the same seats as we'd occupied for almost three months. My mouth was dry and I felt sick with nerves at what we were about to hear and although Ste took my hand to reassure me, I could tell he was worried too. Even Dave looked a bit anxious as we waited for proceedings to start.

The jury foreman stood up to deliver the verdicts and the first name to be read out was Sean Mercer, on a charge of murder.

As soon as I heard 'guilty', I broke down sobbing. Ste, who had tears in his eyes, put his arms round me and I buried my head in his shoulder, to stifle the sobs. But after that, I didn't hear any of the other verdicts. When they had finished, I had to ask Ste what the verdict had been on the rest of them. For me, Mercer was the one I wanted to see brought to justice the most, although Yates came a pretty close second, but I was so overwhelmed with emotion when Mercer was found guilty that I didn't hear anything past that point. It was sheer relief. All I kept thinking was 'At least Rhys has got justice.'

Later, I was told that, when he heard the word 'guilty', Mercer went pale, which was the first time he had shown any emotion at all. His dad, Joseph McCormick, was sitting in the public gallery and he mouthed 'I love you' and started crying, before leaving the court. But up to that point they acted like they couldn't have cared less. Neither of them cared about the death of my son, only about themselves.

Even after all seven of them were found guilty, they couldn't behave. Nathan Quinn cracked a joke and all the others laughed. Then Mercer shook Quinn's hand and hugged him before they were led down to the cells.

After hearing the guilty verdicts, Ste and I stood on the steps outside the court to address the press outside. With his arm round me, Ste bravely made a statement.

'Finally justice has been done for Rhys,' he said. 'Firstly we would like to record our enormous gratitude to the Merseyside Police officers whose professionalism and perseverance secured this outcome, especially Mr Kelly and our family liaison officers.

'From the day Rhys died, the kindness shown to us by the people of Liverpool has been immeasurable. For this we will always thank you from the bottom of our hearts. Over the months we've found strength in the messages of support from many thousands of strangers around the world. For us as a family today this is not the final chapter in this tragedy. But now, at least we can begin the challenge of rebuilding our lives. Thank you all very much.'

Dave also addressed the press. He said: 'Since the senseless murder of Rhys Jones, this family has suffered untold grief and distress.

'Nothing will bring Rhys back but we hope that they will find some peace in the fact that justice has been done.

'Mercer's conduct showed total disregard for Rhys and others. It is fair to say that since the killing of Rhys, Sean Mercer has shown no remorse whatsoever. We only hope that this verdict will bring home the enormity of what he's done and the pain and suffering he has caused.'

The following day, we were back in court for the sentencing and once more holding our breath. Now Mercer had been found guilty, the judge completely changed his tune and really laid into him, as well as praising us. Dave, it seemed, had been right about his motives for telling me off for being emotional while letting them misbehave.

'Rhys Jones died at your hands,' he told Mercer. 'It was a waste of a promising young life.

'His parents' dignity throughout this process has been deeply impressive to all those who have seen them. But it is clear their composure conceals searing emotions.'

Dave and Helen had told us that Mercer was looking at fifteen years, which had seemed a very short sentence to us. So when the judge sentenced him to twenty-two years we were surprised but also very pleased. Even more so when he explained that, even after the twenty-two years were up, Mercer may not be released.

'The tariff I set is not the years you will serve,' he said. 'It is the years you must serve before you can even be considered for release.

'This offence arose from the stupid brutal gang conflict that has struck this part of Liverpool. It is clear you gloried in it. You are not soldiers, you have no discipline, training or honour. You cannot tell the difference between respect and fear. You are stupid shallow criminals. You fired at your intended victims from seventy yards across a pub car park. You aimed shots with murderous intent, as the jury has found. Rhys died because of your brutality and because you are a coward. You proved a coward again. You did not admit what you had done.'

He added that he was satisfied that Mercer had set out to kill and that he had then launched a 'systematic attempt' to destroy evidence and conceal his crime, and he said he wanted the sentence to act as a deterrent to youngsters wanting to join gangs.

'You will not emerge from prison at the very earliest, for a very long time,' he concluded.

One of the things, we believe, that sealed Mercer's fate, and added years to his sentence, was the third shot. As Neil Flewitt had highlighted in his closing speech, he had fired in the other gang's direction, then he fired in Rhys's direction and Rhys hit the floor but then he fired again. Because he saw what he'd done and he still fired another shot, it made it worse, if that's possible, and it counted against him.

Dave, who had devoted sixteen months of his life to getting Mercer in the dock, was happy with the sentence. 'I really didn't think he was going to get that long,' he told us. Helen was also happy and especially pleased that the judge had stipulated it was the minimum sentence he would serve, rather than one of those that can get halved in the long run.

'I've never known anyone on a minimum sentence that long to get out when they have served it,' she told me. 'Chances are he'll be in for a good few years longer.'

Talking to Dave after the sentencing, I asked him how soon after the shooting he had known Mercer was the killer.

'I knew after a week that he was guilty as hell,' he told us. 'I wish I could have told you then but it wouldn't have been right.'

'I'm glad you didn't,' I said. 'It was better that you had the evidence first. I'm just pleased we got the result we did today.' We couldn't thank Dave enough for all he'd done to get that conviction.

After Mercer, Gary Kays and Melvin Coy, the older members of the gang, were each sentenced to seven years for perverting the course of justice.

The other gang members, through their barristers, asked to be sentenced after some reports were carried out and as it was getting so close to Christmas, their sentencing hearing was set for 29 January, so we had over a month to wait to find out what they got. But, as Mercer had received such a long sentence, we were confident they would be given the harshest sentences available. It turned out not to be the case, though, and for one of them in particular it was a joke.

After the verdict on Mercer, we found out the true extent of his feral behaviour, even before Rhys's shooting. In the four years before, he had been stopped by police eighty times and had a conviction for possession of a CS canister and cannabis. Just a few weeks before he killed Rhys, he had been given an ASBO (Anti-Social Behaviour Order) for terrorising staff and security guards at Croxteth Sports Centre and, two months before the shooting, he had ridden a motorbike into the Norris Green 'territory' and had been waving a gun about.

We also found out that, when a big screen was set up in Croxteth to show the *Crimewatch* appeal, where I was pleading for his mum to turn him in and tell the truth, he came cycling up to it. After making sure the police had seen him, he had laughed at them before cycling away.

Mercer's actions clearly showed he was not only out of control but that he thought he was above the law, and would always get away with it. My reaction to all we heard was pure disgust and anger. How could he behave like that, even after he'd killed an innocent, loving boy of eleven? To me he was just scum. I was so full of anger and hatred for Mercer but at least I could be satisfied that he would be locked up for a long, long time, so that was something.

A lot of people are surprised when I say I don't believe in the death penalty, but it's true, even now. I don't believe anyone has the right to take somebody else's life. I believe if you kill, you should go to jail and stay in jail. And never get out. That would be what I would want for Mercer.

People often argue that it costs a lot of money to keep anyone in jail for life, but I still don't think you have the right to take a life, even that of a murderer. I have always felt that way, even before Rhys was murdered, and I haven't changed my view. The way our justice system works, twenty-two years is a good tab for Mercer because that is the minimum he'll serve but ideally I'd like to lock him up for ever and throw away the key.

After the verdicts, we went for a drink with Dave and others in his team. The pubs in the city centre were packed with revellers, full of the Christmas spirit and having a great time, but for us, despite the verdict, it wasn't a celebratory drink. It was a way to let off steam and to relieve the stress that we'd been through but, to be honest, it was a hollow victory.

Granted, we had got the right result but it was a result we never ever wanted in the first place because we never wanted to be there. More than anything, we would have loved to have been home with Rhys, rather than going off for a drink to celebrate the fact that someone had been convicted for his murder. It wouldn't bring Rhys back and it did nothing to ease the agony we would face every single day of the rest of our lives.

That second Christmas we decided to celebrate a bit more, even though my heart wasn't in it. Unlike the previous year, I did put a tree up, albeit a black one I went and bought in Next. To be honest it wasn't very nice – in fact it was horrible – but it reflected how I felt about Christmas without Rhys.

As always, I decorated the tree. Ste's not very artistic when it comes to things like that, so I won't let him anywhere near it in case it ends up looking a mess. Apart from that, though, we didn't put up much decoration. We normally put things in the window, garlands and tinsel and a few little reindeer around the house, but that year we had the bare minimum and what I did put up was only for Owen's sake.

We did still make sure Owen had a pile of presents under the tree, with the usual streamers and chocolate coins. It would have been unfair not to do that for him. We wanted Christmas to be good for him, even though we were all still grieving. It's Owen's Christmas and we had to make it a celebratory time but it was definitely a muted celebration.

On Christmas Day, after spending the morning at the cemetery, we went over to my sister's for the day. We've always taken it in turns to host Christmas but it was, and is still, a case of 'If I turn up, I do and if I don't turn up, I don't.' Luckily Debra understands that. She knows that after going to see Rhys in the morning, I have no idea whether I will be up for the idea of Christmas dinner, pulling crackers and trying to have fun. It's one of the most painful days of the year and I miss him for every minute of it.

That Christmas it was hard to keep my mind off the sentencing of the four remaining boys, and particularly James Yates. We were grateful that Mercer had been sentenced before the Christmas break, so at least that wasn't hanging over our heads, and we were fairly certain we knew what the tariff was going to be because Helen had talked us through it. She said that for the possession of a gun it was five years max, and that assisting an offender would be a lot less than that. The only thing that was a bit off-putting was that she warned us that they often take off the time already served. Also, she said, most people don't serve the full term. So if you get five years for a gun offence you are only going to serve two and a half, unless you really screw up in prison.

Although we were furious about the way the others had behaved, both in the attempts to save Mercer's neck and in court, Yates was the one we were most concerned about. From what we'd heard in court, and learned from Dave, he was a real nasty piece of work and, if he hadn't handed that gun to Mercer earlier that day, our son would still be alive.

After New Year, there was a four-week wait while the reports on the remaining defendants were filed and, on 29 January, we were called back to court to hear the sentencing of Nathan Quinn, Dean Kelly, Boy M and James Yates.

Filing back into the courtroom, I felt the knot of anxiety in my stomach that I had felt every day of the tense eleven-week trial. I worried they would get off too lightly, that Yates, in particular, would get a lenient sentence. Although the lads in the dock looked tense, they still had their cocky front on, laughing and joking as if they were facing nothing more serious than a telling off from a grumpy headmaster.

Quinn, who was eighteen, got a year but it turned out that he was already serving a five-year sentence for gun crime. His sentence for assisting an offender was added on to the end. The judge said he was obviously 'an active gang member' and he added, 'Your aggression levels are clearly high. You have nine proven adjudications against you in prison. Six of them for fighting or assault.'

Because of his age Dean Kelly, who was seventeen, had been referred to as Boy K in the press throughout the trial but the judge lifted the restriction after he was found guilty. He got four years for assisting an offender and two counts of possession of a firearm, because he had moved the murder weapon to Boy X's loft, days after the killing. Judge Irwin said, 'By Sunday twenty-sixth [August], the killing was all over the estate and the country. In the middle of that outcry you moved the weapon. You are at significant risk of reoffending and causing harm to the public.'

Even so, once his remand had been taken into account, he only had fifteen months to serve, which didn't seem a lot to us.

With Boy M, the judge was lenient because he was only sixteen and had ADHD (attention deficit and hyperactivity disorder). He got a two-year supervision order and a four-month curfew and, given that he had been driven to becoming a hermit after being beaten up for being a 'grass', I think the judge was fair. He wouldn't have got involved if they hadn't come straight to his house and he was too afraid of them to grass them up again. But for us, I suppose, it was lucky that they had come to him and that his mum had been brave enough to stand up and tell the court that they had.

The biggest shock was when the judge passed sentence on James Yates, who I blamed much more than the others. He had supplied the gun and encouraged Mercer to go out and shoot the 'Nogga Dogz' that night. If he hadn't had his leg in plaster after crashing a quad bike, he would probably have been the one on that bike with a gun. Looking at him, and the way he behaved, I thought he was pure evil, through and through.

When the police went to arrest him, in April 2008, he was at his girlfriend Leanne Morrey's house and he broke his ankle jumping out of a window to escape the coppers. He even proposed to Leanne in the first days of the trial and she came to court wearing a new engagement ring. Why anyone would want to marry a scumbag like him is beyond me. He's a horrible, evil person.

The judge put Yates in the witness stand and we held our breath. Then he said, 'For possession and supply of firearms, I sentence you to seven years.' He was also given two six-year terms for assisting an offender – but they were set to run concurrently, meaning a total of seven years. He was so chuffed with that he even punched the air and whooped in celebration. He knew he had got off too easy and he was made up because if you get seven years, you'll be out in three and half.

All that meant that after time on remand was deducted Yates would serve just two years and nine months, so it was a joke as far as we were concerned.

Ste and I looked at each other in horror. We couldn't believe he had only got seven years. As soon as we heard the judge pronounce his sentence, Dave Kelly flushed with anger and shook his head.

'No, we're not having that,' he said. 'No way.' Angry tears fell from my eyes and I broke down, but Ste put his arms round me.

'Don't worry about it Mel,' he said quietly. 'Dave said we are going to appeal.'

But worse was to come. In the dock, Quinn, Kelly and Yates were cock-a-hoop – laughing, cheering and winking at family members in the courtroom, including Yates' lying parents. Then, as he was walking down the steps to go back to the cells, Yates said, as loud as you like, 'All this for some fucking kid!'

With all the kerfuffle going on in the dock, I hadn't heard it but Dave bristled and Ste's face looked like thunder.

'Did you hear what he just said?' Ste said, in a furious voice. When he repeated it I was livid. How could he be so disrespectful, even now?

'Why doesn't the judge call him back up?' I said. 'Why did they let them get away with stuff like that?' I thought he should have been dragged back up and told, 'I just heard what you said. Now you're getting another five years on top.' I guess that's not how it works in the legal system though. We still had a few more hoops to jump through before justice would really be done.

As soon as we left the courtroom, Dave and Helen were keen to talk it through with us.

'That's not long enough,' said Dave. 'He's not getting away with that.'

'Just appeal,' said Helen. She explained that if we, and the prosecution, felt that the sentence was too lenient, we could take the matter to the court of appeal in London. 'The sentences were what I expected for each individual offence,' she explained. 'But the sentences don't have to run concurrently.'

We all agreed that we should lodge an appeal and, in the meantime, we issued a statement to the press.

It read: 'We are disgusted at the seven-year sentence given to Sean Mercer's accomplice, James Yates, today. In our minds he is the one who provided the gun that killed our son and he deserved a longer sentence. We feel seven years is a disgrace.

'However we hope the other sentences handed out today, and before Christmas, do send a clear message to all those involved in gangs and with guns that they will be found out, tracked down, convicted and heavily sentenced. Despite this, these sentences can in no way compensate for the loss of our loving son who had the world and his future at his feet.

'Since the conviction and sentencing of Sean Mercer before Christmas we have slowly returned to some sort of normal day-to-day life – but our lives will never ever be the same without Rhys. It is us who are serving the life sentence, and we face that every day.'

Less than four weeks later, on 24 February, it was announced that Vera Baird QC, the solicitor general, had referred the case to the court of appeal. A statement from the attorney general, Baroness Scotland, said: 'If the court of appeal decides that the sentence is unduly lenient they have the power to increase the length of the sentence.'

The hearing was set for October 2009, eight months away. In the meantime, Dave told us, 'Now I'm going after the parents as well, Yates' parents and Mercer's mum. We'll get them for perverting the course of justice.'

Throughout the trial I had been saying to Ste, 'The two most evil people in that dock are Mercer and Yates, and you only have to look at their parents to see why they're like that.'

Both Yates' parents and Mercer's mum knew exactly what their sons had done and did everything they could to cover it up. Janette Mercer lied and lied, while Francis and Marie Yates destroyed evidence and Francis even tried to provide Mercer with a false alibi. What kind of example did they set their sons? It doesn't get any worse than murder, so how could you cover that up? How could you look your son in the face and know what he'd done, that he killed an innocent eleven-year-old? I can't comprehend it.

In the original trial, as well as the tape of Yates' parents burning the sim card, various recordings from the police probe in their house had been played. Even after all that we'd heard, one shocked me to the core. Marie Yates, a mother of three, was heard discussing the shooting and saying, 'Oh my good God, brave isn't it? Whoever has done it has a lot of bottle.'

Everyone in the public gallery gasped when they heard it and I felt like someone had punched me in the stomach. 'Brave!' I thought. 'How can shooting a defenceless little boy on his way home from football practice be brave?' I hadn't thought anything could make me more angry than I already was but fury bubbled up inside me at those words. To say that anyone who killed a child had 'a lot of bottle' just highlighted what sort of family they were. No normal parent could ever say that about such a devastating, senseless act of violence.

The jury had also heard other conversations between the family, including one about how Francis Yates had picked up his son and Mercer shortly after they had destroyed the evidence, and taken them to a secluded spot to talk about the murder.

Later, on 27 August, five days after the murder, he was heard talking to Marie and telling her what he knew.

He said: 'When we went away, me and James, with him [Mercer] we sat and discussed. All we were discussing had nothing to do with James, nothing to do with me. James asked me to try to get Mercer out of trouble. James asked me "Can you try to get Sean out of trouble?" and I went "I will do as much as I can", so I asked the two of them "What's gone on?" And they told me.'

'You come home and told me no one knows,' Marie replied. 'All fucking Crocky knows.' On that same night, Marie decided to burn her son's sim card, to cover up his connection with other Crocky Crew members.

On 1 September, while the police were still searching for a murder weapon, Yates and his dad discussed where the gun had been hidden. He asked about the gun in the 'lad's house' and added, 'What if it got raided?'

'Well, it will never get raided,' James Yates told him. 'If it does they will only search his room.'

Later Francis Yates was talking to his wife about what he would say if Mercer told the police that 'James knows everything and Franny gave me the alibi.'

'If anyone comes and says that, I will deny it,' he said.

He also told her, 'I think our James went with them to dump the stuff and douse him in petrol ...,' proving he had in-depth knowledge of exactly what went on the night Rhys died.

In a separate recording, he seemed to be suggesting that Mercer had no hope of getting away with this.

'Mercer now, he's not thick,' he said. 'He's a clever kid. He knows he is fucked. He should go and say "All right" and tell a story – "Yeah I got a phone call. I'm not prepared to tell you who it was off ... I stormed out, went and got a gun and Bang! End of."'

When Dave had originally told us, 'I'm not just going after them. I'm going after the parents as well,' I admit I thought it would be hard to pin anything on them.

But having heard all the evidence, I could see it was clear how deeply involved they were and they must have known they were in over their heads. The Yateses both put in a guilty plea and in February, when her case came to the magistrates' court, Janette Mercer changed her plea to guilty as well.

Because of the guilty pleas, this trial was mercifully short and we were in court again in April to hear the sentencing. Janette Mercer's lawyer said she wanted to 'apologise most sincerely for what she did' and he begged the judge to suspend her sentence for the sake of her young son and her sick parents. Not surprisingly, that made my blood boil again. What about *my* son and *my* family? What consideration had she shown any of us? Now she was asking to get off scot-free so she could look after *her* family when mine had been ripped to shreds. How dare she!

Luckily, the judge was having none of it and he jailed her for three years for perverting the course of justice. 'Your son was a key suspect in the murder and you knew he had told a pack of lies,' he said. 'You backed him up and you told more lies.'

Both the Yateses were given four and a half years for perverting the course of justice and Francis was given an extra three years on top for helping to establish a false alibi.

The judge blasted all three of them for holding back the police investigation while 'the grieving family and friends of Rhys Jones anxiously waited for justice.'

'Each of you, acting as you did, was misleading the police in relation to their inquiry, frustrating their investigation into the murder, diminishing the prospect of detection, wasting valuable police time in undermining the whole process of criminal justice,' Judge Globe said. 'Rhys's murder has left in its wake shock, devastation, heartache and emptiness among his family and friends. It's saddened the lives and touched the hearts of all decent people who live in Merseyside and beyond.'

I hadn't imagined they would all get a custodial sentence and, hearing the judgement, I was glad that Dave had pushed to get them charged and sentenced. They truly deserved it. We were told that James Yates broke down in tears when he heard what they had got. That's probably the only time he showed any emotion about any of it.

Standing outside the court, after the hearing, Ste told the waiting press how we both felt about the three parents.

'In our eyes Mrs Mercer and Mr and Mrs Yates have always been as guilty as their sons. As adults they should have known right from wrong. They knew of the terrible crimes their children had committed.

'They should have done everything in their power to bring them to justice. To cover up Rhys's murder and to protect a murderer and his accomplices and prolong our agony is unforgivable. As parents themselves they should have understood our pain but they chose to ignore it. For us no prison sentence for these people would be long enough.'

'Unforgivable' is exactly how I still see their actions. They got out of prison years ago now, but I could never forgive their callous actions, not for as long as I live.

While another fight on our road to justice was over, there was still one more fight to get through – our bid to get Yates' sentence increased.

In October 2009, we travelled down to London with Dave and his colleague DI Martin Leahy and got a taxi to the court of appeal, which is housed at the Royal Courts of Justice, in the Strand. The huge Gothic building, with its church-style windows and grey stone statues of Jesus, Solomon and Alfred the Great, was instantly recognisable from hundreds of news reports, when I'd watched people involved in trials talking to the press outside or just being pictured going in and out. I have to say it impressed me because to me it is a 'proper' court.

Inside, the lobby, or Great Hall, is magnificent, like a huge cathedral with stunning mosaic marbled floors, coats of arms and a vaulted roof eighty feet high. The courtrooms are panelled in dark wood with old-fashioned, raised platforms for judges and when you walk along the floor, the old boards creak through years of use. It's all quite intimidating and imposing, and I remember thinking 'I wish all courts were still like this.'

These days the more modern courts, like the now familiar Liverpool Crown Court, are more like offices and when you walk in you don't feel like you're in a court of law or feel in awe of your surroundings. Maybe they don't want people to feel that intimidated any more but I prefer those courts that are really old-fashioned and imposing. Perhaps people like Mercer and his gang would have shown more respect in such daunting surroundings, but I doubt it.

Whether it was down to the courtroom or the fact he was facing this one on his own, Yates was very quiet during his appeal, much more subdued than he had been at the original trial. He wasn't as cocky because he had no one to show off to, and no mates to muck about with. He just stood there meekly and didn't look over at us once. I don't think he was any more intimidated than he had been before – I don't think any of them would have been – but he was trying to be on his best behaviour so he didn't get any more years added and he had probably been warned by his lawyer that repeating the disgusting antics of the last time wouldn't do him any favours.

Like with the previous trial, I was really nervous and convinced it wasn't going to go our way, so I was relieved when the judge agreed that the sentence was 'unduly lenient.'

He said gun crime was a 'modern pestilence' that claims 'innocent victims.'

'The law is clear,' he added. 'If you choose to be loyal to a gang member who has committed murder you must, if convicted, expect a substantial prison sentence.'

When he told Yates his sentence would be increased by five years, to a total of twelve, Yates looked down and shook his head and I just started crying uncontrollably. I sobbed my heart out. To me, he's the most evil one of the whole lot of them and I was happy in the sense that it was the maximum sentence that they could have given him, for that crime, but not in the sense that I think it's long enough. I don't think he should ever have got out again. It's the same with Mercer. People say, 'He got a good sentence,' and I agree he did, but only in respect of the justice system as it is now. If they changed it, and I had my way, they'd both rot in jail. Sadly, apart from Mercer, they are all out of jail now.

# CHAPTER NINE

# A Family Lost

**ALTHOUGH STE AND** I had told the world, after the trial, that we had 'slowly returned to some sort of normal day-to-day life', it was far from the truth as far as I was concerned. In the wake of the original trial, Ste had once more returned to work but I sank even further into the depths of depression.

While we had been going to court, and because of the length of time the court case took, over eleven weeks, we had something to focus on. To be honest, we had been focusing on that result since the day that Rhys died, because all we wanted was justice, for the people who did this to be put behind bars. When all that stopped, and we had the sentencing we wanted, I had imagined I would be happier, that I would feel some form of closure, but that's not what happened.

We couldn't be happy and jubilant because nothing was going to bring Rhys back, not even putting his killer away for life. So after the trial, when once again people went back to their own lives and their own families, it was like a huge void opened up and I fell into it.

In the wake of the trial, lots of people in the public eye, such as the leader of the City Council and even the Prime Minister, Gordon Brown, had commented on the verdict. One local councillor, Marilyn Fielding, said, 'The local community can now finally draw a line under the events of August 2007 and begin to move on.' But that was the problem. Everyone else could move on, but we couldn't. Our happy family life had been shattered and could never be put together again.

Although I have no time for any of the politicians who spouted their views on Rhys's murder and Mercer's conviction, David Cameron, then leader of the opposition, came closest to the truth.

'With the conviction of Sean Mercer and other gang members, justice at least has been done,' he said. 'But for Rhys's parents, Stephen and Melanie, the hurt will never end.'

Now, as depression overwhelmed me, I could see nothing but darkness and pain ahead. How could we have a future without Rhys? I began to feel suicidal and I honestly felt like I had nothing left to live for. Of course I had Owen and Ste, but I was in such a deep depression I couldn't see a way out of it. I missed Rhys so deeply, every day, and I couldn't see how I could live without him. There were so many times I felt that I just couldn't go on and it was only the thought of putting Owen and Ste through even more pain that stopped me from acting on that.

When it comes to depression, people are always full of advice, and friends and family were telling me to go out and have a walk, and various other things they thought would make me feel better. But in that frame of mind, how are you supposed to do that? I just wanted to sit indoors and do nothing, and that's exactly what I did.

Most of the time I sat on the couch, eating junk food and watching mindless telly. Sometimes Debra would come round and force me to shower and get dressed, or make me something healthy for lunch, but it didn't make me feel any better. Rhys was gone. His killer was in jail. What was the point in carrying on?

One day I told Debra, 'I just feel like I've got nothing left to live for any more.' 'Don't say that,' she said, although she could tell I was serious.

'Why not? It's true,' I said. 'At least with the investigation and the trial we had something to focus on. Now even that's gone. Now there's just nothing but his empty bedroom upstairs.'

I knew Ste was worried, and he tried to help, but there was nothing he could do. After a few weeks, Ste said he'd spoken to the managers at Tesco and that they said if I wanted to go back, I could choose my hours.

'Why don't you go back and just do an hour or two,' he said.

'Why would I want to go back to work?' I asked him.

'Getting into a routine and getting out of the house might help,' he said. 'You night start to feel a bit more normal.'

'I don't want to feel normal,' I snapped at him. 'Nothing will ever be normal again.'

In the black depths of my despair, I felt like no one could understand my pain and I struggled to see how the rest of the world could just carry on with their lives. Obviously Ste was hurting just as much but, as he could get up and go to work and still function as a human being, I couldn't always see that.

Eventually, after a lot of gentle nudging from Debra and Ste, I went to the doctor. I had always been adamant that I wouldn't go down the medication route, but counselling clearly wasn't for me and I didn't know where else to turn. I was so desperate that I gave in and started taking antidepressants, which I was on and off for years after that.

Slowly, I began to feel like I could carry on, that I had to carry on for the sake of Owen and for Rhys. He wouldn't have wanted to see me like this and I needed to find a way to start living some sort of life again, even if it could never be the happy life I had before. Then one day, in February 2009, I suddenly decided I needed to get back to work. I thought 'If I don't go back now, I'm never going to go back.' I had been off for two years, although it didn't feel like it, and I don't think anyone thought I was ever going to work again.

Initially I went back for an hour a day, then two. I worked my way back in gradually. Tesco were brilliant, and continued to pay my full wages even when I went back on reduced hours, but even doing an hour a day was tough, I admit.

Over the years I have made a lot of good friends at the store, and I had seen them in the time I had been off. Some had come to Rhys's funeral and to sit in the public gallery during the trial, to show their support, and they were brilliant when I returned to work. They were happy to talk to me about how I was coping, if I wanted to talk, but they also acted completely normal around me when we weren't talking about it. The rest of the staff, the ones I wasn't so close to, just didn't know what to say initially but I can understand that.

People have often said to me, 'You're like a celebrity,' and, to be honest, I really hate it. I was forced into the public gaze by a horrible tragedy in my life but I've never been comfortable with that. Friends have commented on how often I change my hair but there's a reason I'm always changing it, and it's to try to be anonymous, because even now perfect strangers come up to me and offer sympathetic words all the time. The fact that everyone knew about Rhys made my return to work so much more difficult. I worked on the checkouts, so I dealt with the public every day, and there would be long queues on my till while the other tills would be empty. People just wanted to come to my till to express their sympathy, or give me a hug, which I couldn't bear.

Everyone meant well, of course, but it took all my strength to get up and ready to go to work in the morning, and then someone would put an arm round me, or say something sympathetic, and I'd just break down. Every day, customers would come up and say, 'Can I hug you?' and I'd be trying to back away from them behind the till and saying, 'No, sorry, I'm a bit fragile.'

Quite often, other members of staff would try to disperse the queue, and tell the shoppers, 'There's an empty till here.' But nine times out of ten they'd say, 'No it's OK. We'll wait here.'

Head office tried to help, and offered me a role in the back room doing the wages, so that I wouldn't have to face the public all day, but all my friends were on the tills and I didn't want to be alone in the back room. If I'd wanted to be on my own all day, I could have stayed at home. Instead, I decided, I had to get used to the pitying looks and sympathetic noises.

Whenever I had a day off my friend Donna would tell me that people came up to her till and asked after me. She used to do an impression of them, tilting her head and saying, 'Aww. How *is* Mel?' and she would make me howl with laughter. It felt good that I could still have a laugh with my closest friends, and it helped me to be with them again.

One small thing that had also changed when I went back was my constant charging of my phone. Since the day Rhys died, when I couldn't phone Ste, I have never, ever let my phone run out of charge. I carry a charger around everywhere and I would get told off at work because I was plugging my phone in all the time, but I can't ever let that happen again.

That summer, shortly before the second anniversary of Rhys's death, was when we found the carved RJ-07 on the old leylandii. We were surprised that Rhys would have done something like that, because we thought he would have deemed it a bit naughty, but it touched us because he'd left his mark.

'I never knew he'd done that,' said Ste, smiling fondly. 'I used to do the same all the time when I was a kid. There are a few trees in the grounds of Fazakerley Hospital with my initials on.'

It turned out that wasn't the only marker Rhys had left around the garden. After that we also found a few scrawlings of his and Owen's initials on the downpipe on the back of the house, where it had faded in the sun.

When we had the tree cut down, about five years later, we asked them to cut out the piece that had RJ-07 carved into it so we could keep it. You can't really make it out now, as it's faded, but RJ-07 is indelibly carved into my heart.

Nearly two years on, the pain was still unbearable. A find like the carving on the tree could set me back and reduce me to a sobbing mess, all over again. Rhys's empty chair at the dining room table or his quiet, empty bedroom could set me off. Every time I saw kids on the estate playing outside, or kicking a football about, I thought 'Rhys should be out there with them.' The Farm's 'All Together Now' – that had played on a loop in the funeral parlour – came on the radio and I would be inconsolable all over again.

Ste was still suffering too, although he rarely voiced it. At Goodison Park, the theme tune, 'Johnny Todd', would upset him and he would look at the dads with their young sons and think, 'Why isn't that us?' He missed mucking about with Rhys, sneaking up on him with his video camera to catch him on film doing something daft. He even missed wandering around the estate looking for him because his tea was ready.

We both had good days and bad days but there was never a day when we didn't think about Rhys constantly – and the same is true today.

To make matters worse, we were set to face Mercer in court once more. Just a week into January, and before the others had even been sentenced, Mercer had lodged an appeal against both his conviction and his sentence. We were told that the appeal would have to be heard and that the date had been set for September, at the court of appeal in London.

Both Ste and I were fuming. Not only had that scumbag tried everything he could to stop the police catching him, putting us through eight months of hell in the process, but when he was finally found guilty he lodged an appeal straight away, meaning we would have to face him in court again.

We had been warned that he would be allowed to lodge an appeal if he wanted to, within four weeks of the verdict, but we were still a bit surprised that he was going to go ahead with it. It meant the worry set in again and we were thinking, 'If he thinks he's got a chance of appealing then what's going to happen?' We'd just been through all that heartache and if he did get appeal, we wondered, what form would it take?

We were convinced he had no case for a reduction in his sentence, as he'd blocked the police at every turn and had never admitted his guilt. Even so, the thought of dragging the whole thing up again in court was horrendous.

When it came to it, although we don't know this for sure, we think he must have been advised he had no hope of winning and that his sentence might even be increased. We can only assume someone with some common sense talked to him because a week before we were due to go down to London, he dropped the appeal. The fact that he waited until the last minute, knowing that was hanging over our heads after all we'd been through, shows how callous he really is.

*

After a couple of years of living with my memories, and the emptiness that Rhys had left behind, I came to the conclusion that we should move house. I felt that staying on the estate, round the corner from the very car park where he had been shot, was not helping us cope with our grief. Because of the way that the estate is laid out, there's no way of getting to the shops or the doctor's surgery without passing the Fir Tree.

Shortly after Rhys's death, the pub had been raided and shut down because the police found evidence of drug dealing and gang activity. Eventually it did reopen, under new management, who put a new fence around it, spent a bit of money on it and changed its name back to the Stand Farm, but it soon closed again. It doesn't really matter what you call it. It's still the same pub and it's still the same car park and it will be a good few years before people get over the apprehension of going there.

The trouble was that I couldn't get away from it. If I wanted to go to the doctor's, I had to walk past that pub. If I wanted to go to the shops, I had to walk past that pub. I felt we needed a fresh start, and to move away, but Ste didn't.

Over the years this was to become a sticking point with us because Ste wanted to stay and never move. To Ste,

Rhys is in this house and evidence of him is all around – from the tree carving to the dents in the garage door. Rhys's bedroom still lay silent and untouched, with its Everton posters and duvet, and most of his things were still in the cupboards. Ste felt that moving would be like abandoning Rhys, somehow.

When I first brought it up, Ste was adamant and gave me a point blank 'No.' Eventually, after lot of emotional conversations, I thought I'd talked him round and he even agreed to get an estate agent to come to look at the house.

A really nice lady came over to give us a valuation, and she obviously knew who we were. When she saw Rhys's room she looked a little uncomfortable.

'I don't want to upset you or anything but you'll have to decorate this room,' she said, kindly. 'You'll get all kinds of ghouls coming, just wanting to have a look and take a photo of Rhys's bedroom.'

Over the years, I had kept that room out of the public eye, even though the press wanted a photo of Rhys's bedroom. We must have been asked about a hundred times, but I always said no. I wouldn't let them in my house. This is our home, this is private, and Rhys's room was his private space. Because it was such a part of Rhys, I hadn't wanted to change a thing but she was right when she said we would have to do it if we were going to put the house on the market.

Together, Ste and I sorted out all Rhys's stuff and we kept most of it, boxed up and stored under our bed. Over the years he had built up quite a collection of Star Wars figures and wrestler figures, which we divvied up between his closest mates on the close. We told them, 'If you want them, you can have them,' and they were made up with them so they went to good homes.

The bed and the little wardrobe we just binned because there wasn't much point in keeping them, and we finally retrieved all the socks on the top of the wardrobe where he'd rolled them up and booted them.

Sorting out all his stuff, the things he loved, was really emotional and there were a lot of tears. We ended up keeping more than we binned because I couldn't bear the thought of chucking it away. We still have all his football kits – we counted 27 kits that he had amassed over the years because he never threw them out. I couldn't help but smile when I remembered how Rhys used to put his old Everton shirts on the dog when they were playing in the garden. Lennox loved joining in the football, running after the ball and jumping for it and, in the summer, Rhys would get his bubble machine out and the dog would have hours of fun chasing the bubbles.

As well as his kits, we kept quite a few of his posters, including the Rooney photo on the wall that he had poked the eyes out of. Some of his things, like his remote-controlled car and the big stuffed gorilla that he had refused to be parted with, went up into the loft but most of it is still stored under our bed and his bike and skateboard are still in the garage.

After we'd cleared it out, Ste took down the Everton border that went round the walls and then stripped the wallpaper and painted the room. In the end, I think, it was good that we were forced to redecorate because it made us deal with it, rather than endlessly putting it off because it was too upsetting to face. It was a hard decision to make. It felt like another part of Rhys being taken away but it had to be done at some point. We couldn't keep it as a shrine for ever. After Ste had finished, we were both pretty down but the effect on Ste was that he changed his mind completely about moving.

'I can't do it Mel,' he said. 'We can't leave all the memories of Rhys behind and move away.' So in the end we decided not to sell the house.

Ironically, a short while after that, Ste dropped a bombshell.

It was early one morning, in July 2011, and I was standing in the bedroom drying my hair when he came in from his night shift. Normally, when he comes home, he strips off his uniform and gets straight in the shower, but on this occasion he came straight into the bedroom and lay on the bed, fully clothed. Thinking that was odd, I looked at him and I could tell by his face that something was wrong.

'What's up?' I asked.

'I'm leaving,' he said, bluntly.

'What?' I said, not comprehending what he was telling me. 'What do you mean you're leaving?'

'I'm leaving,' he repeated. 'I've got a flat. It's all organised.'

'You can't leave,' I told him. There was no way I felt I could stand on my own two feet, after all that had happened.

'I'm not going for good,' he said. 'I just need to be alone so I can sort my head out. I can't handle it any more. I need some time and space and I can't get that here.'

He said he was having trouble handling the situation and that he felt everything he was doing was wrong.

I was devastated. I knew there were problems with our marriage – there were bound to be. After all, we'd both suffered the worst loss a parent can suffer. But I didn't think things were that bad. I knew there was nobody else involved. It was purely down to what we had both been through and the way we were dealing with it, as individuals, but I was still shocked.

I thought back to what the FLO had said, that couples never survive a tragic loss like ours, and I thought, 'Oh God, maybe she was right.' I had to admit things had been going downhill since the trial. When we lost Rhys we had so much to focus on, we weren't really dealing with our emotions or our relationship. After the funeral there was a dip, but we knew we needed to be together, we needed to be focused because of the police investigation and then through the trial. But after the trial, things began to fall apart.

Ste and I sort of knew things weren't right between us, but in the midst of misery people grieve differently and, as I've said, we are like chalk and cheese when it comes to emotions. If I'm upset, everyone knows I'm upset and that's the way I am. I like to talk, and talk, and talk, about it. Ste is the complete opposite. He likes to take himself off somewhere, away from everyone, and that's what he was doing.

Although I was desperate for him not to leave I was so emotionally battered at this point, I had no fight left in me.

'OK, fine,' I said. 'Do whatever. Do whatever you like.'

Ste packed his stuff and left straight away and it was only after the door closed that I totally broke down. He'd said it wasn't for ever but I didn't know if he was going to come back. How could I know?

As well as being upset, I was angry because I felt like he was leaving me *and* Owen. We'd both already lost Rhys and now if felt like we were losing him too. But I could see he needed to do something because he just wasn't dealing with his grief at all. He wouldn't speak to anyone about that.

That summer, as he was about to enter his third year at Hope University, Owen had already made plans to move out as well. Although his university was in Liverpool, he and his mates had decided to get a flat in the city.

'It will cost you a fortune,' I had told him when he first mentioned it.

'I know but I want the full uni experience,' he reasoned. 'Most people don't live at home when they go to uni.'

'If that's what you want, that's fine by us,' I said. I completely understood that he wanted to spread his wings a little and I was just grateful he would still be on the doorstep.

Even so, after Ste's announcement, I knew that Owen would feel protective of me and when I told him his dad had gone, he reacted as I had thought he would.

'Mum, I won't move out,' he said. 'I'll stay here with you.'

'No, Owen,' I said. 'You will move out. You're not changing your plans because of this.'

'What if Dad doesn't come back?' he asked.

'If your dad doesn't come back then he doesn't come back,' I said. 'I'm fine. I can deal with it. You can't put your life on hold. Unless you're going to stay here until I die, you need to go. You need to have your own life.'

At that point, I could see he was getting upset and he walked out. I broke my heart crying, thinking, 'Oh my God, he thinks he has to stay here for me. I don't want that for him.'

In the end, I managed to persuade him that he should go and he did move out, and into the flat with his friends. Luckily, he was only down the road and he had managed to get a part-time job at my Tesco branch, working evenings, so he would be coming into work just as I was finishing, which meant I saw him a lot in passing.

Naturally, as he was living on the doorstep, I didn't stop doing all the 'mum' stuff either. I would do his washing and do some shopping for him so he had plenty to eat and, as it turned out, I saw plenty of Ste as well. He was home every weekend, because he still took Owen to the Everton game every week and they always met at home first. Then he'd come home on a Sunday morning, have breakfast with me and then we'd go together to Rhys's grave. After that he would bring me back home and go back to his flat. It was like he wasn't there but he was there, which was a comfort to me. It was obvious he didn't want to cut the ties completely, which made me think he probably would come back at some point, but we still weren't really addressing any problems. Although we'd talk when he came down to see me, it was never about anything that mattered.

Although I was living alone for those six months, I wasn't really on my own because people were always popping in. Sometimes, to be honest, I would have liked to be on my own a bit more. Sometimes I would think, 'I can't be bothered to make conversation with anyone.' Don't get me wrong, I am grateful that my friends and family wanted to support me and to pop round to check on me, and everyone around me was brilliant. But when people turn up, you have to make conversation and there were times that I didn't want to. I was in such a deep pit of despair, I just wanted to lie on the couch and vegetate.

At the start of mine and Ste's break I decided that I wasn't going to put any pressure on him to come back, but he knew he could come back if that's what he wanted. And he did. At Christmas, when the lease on the flat was about to run out, he came over and said, 'I want to come back.'

'Yeah fine,' I said. 'Come back.' That was that. There was no standing on ceremony. We slipped straight back into our lives and it felt a bit like he'd just been away for the weekend. But that's just Ste all over.

Even so, I was just glad to have him home. Owen was at uni, and I felt, if Ste and I break up, then what is there? There's nothing left. I have Owen but he's grown up and living his own life, and he can't spend his whole time worrying about me.

It may sound like a cliché but I honestly believe we are stronger together since that break than we ever have been. He needed that time and space and I understand that. A lot of my family didn't understand and said, 'What will you do now? He's left you.' But I knew he just needed some headspace because we were both going through the same thing, just handling it differently. People around you try to understand, and even think they do understand, the situation that you're in, but no one can ever really understand it, ever, until they have been in that situation themselves.

# A Fresh Start

**WITH STE HOME,** and both of us working again, we fell into our old routines. Although nothing would ever be 'normal' again, we had to try to get on with our lives the best we could.

Our families were really supportive and, unlike many other people, didn't find the subject of Rhys an awkward one. Ste's mum talks about Rhys all the time when we go round to see her and that's a good thing, for all of us. If the family didn't talk about Rhys I would probably be falling out with them all. It's nothing forced, it's just what comes up in the conversation. So something will happen and someone will say, 'Rhys would have liked that,' or 'Do you remember when Rhys did that?' It's just natural to talk about him because he was here, and we can't forget that.

In the summer of 2012, Owen graduated with a degree in Computer Science and he decided to stay on at Hope University to study for a Masters. We were happy to support his choice and, as neither of us had gone to university, we were really made up that he had chosen to do that, and had done so well.

When he passed his first degree, we went to a graduation at the Catholic cathedral in Liverpool but for his Master's degree, a year later, the graduation ceremony was at the Anglican cathedral, where Rhys's funeral had been. Being in the cathedral brought back painful memories but seeing Owen dressed up in his graduation gown and mortar board was the proudest moment of my life. Despite all he'd been through, he had achieved so much and, at the same time, he had grown into a lovely young man. He even had letters after his name – MSc. I was so full of pride that I confess I shed a tear or two, but at least they were happy tears.

The fund for the community centre continued to grow with generous donations from many people, including my colleagues at the Tesco branch where I worked, who donated £1,000 in 2010 and had regular charity days to raise more. Once we had raised half the £500,000 required, Liverpool City Council stumped up the rest and donated the land on Croxteth Park estate for it to be built. It was a field at the end of the estate where Ste and I had often walked Lennox in the past. We never let him off the lead because he would never come back, but he loved it there.

So, towards the end of 2012, the plans were all in and ready to go and LCC gave us the green light to start building. In November, Ste and I went along to dig the first piece of turf and, although it had been a long time coming, it was great to have something positive happening in Rhys's name. The estate has a population of thousands and it was crying out for a central point, somewhere kids could take part in sports and other activities.

It was due to open in July 2013 but, in the end, the works were delayed and it finally opened on 31 August. The whole community turned up for the day and Ste and I cut the ribbon on the door at the opening ceremony.

Finally opening the Rhys Jones Community Centre, with the motto 'Hope, Aspiration, Unity', was truly a great day for us. We felt like we had achieved something very special, something that was great for the estate because at last there was somewhere for the kids to go, and it would be Rhys's lasting legacy.

Even so, it was a very emotional experience. It was painful, because Rhys wasn't there, but we were smiling at the same time because we were looking at all the little children running around and playing on all the new pitches and they were so made up with it. While it can't help us get over Rhys, it was nice to see something good come out of something so terrible.

The centre was to have clubs for everyone, from mum and toddler groups and play groups to pensioners, as well as being available for birthday parties and events. For the footballers, we put in all-weather pitches that they can use all year round. That's the bit that Rhys would have loved the most. He would have been out there playing in all weathers.

Once the centre was up and running, Ste and I took a step back and decided we'd done our bit. Raising money is quite draining because there are only so many places to go and people to ask for donations, and there are only so many times you can ask Everton or Liverpool for a signed shirt. It's especially hard for me because I hate asking people for money, even if it is for my son's charity. I just can't do it. So once it was built, we left the day-to-day running to others. The committee runs it really well, but they struggle financially and they still have to try to make money to keep the building going. They get some money from people who pay to use the pitches and hall, but it's only a minimal amount, and there's no government funding.

To be honest, although I am pleased the community centre was opened, I don't go there myself because it is too close to where Rhys was shot, and I hate to go to that part of the estate. It brings back the most horrendous memories and it's all too raw.

We haven't given up helping out altogether. In 2017, they were trying to raise money for new goalposts, which, incredibly, can cost up to £5,000 per pair. I couldn't believe it! So, in August, we took part in the Run For Rhys. Well, actually, Ste ran and I walked.

Between us we took part in three events – one for the little kids, then a 3k, which my sister Debra and I walked, and a 5k, which Ste ran with Dave Kelly. Dave raised £400 on his own. We did a bit of promotion for the runs, to make sure people were aware of them, and the centre planned to make it an annual event, which is good because it does raise much-needed money. But that's all we take part in now.

Over the course of the investigation and the trial, Dave became a close friend and we kept in touch afterwards. Dave often texts Ste saying, 'Do you want to go for a pint?' so they meet up regularly and, as a couple, we often meet with him and his lovely wife Donna. As far as I'm concerned, he is a hero. Every time I see him I give him a big hug. He must think 'Here she is again!' I always say to Donna, 'I love your husband, you know.' She just laughs and says, 'You're mad.' But, for getting those eleven people convicted, he'll always be my hero.

Sadly, it seemed his boss at Merseyside Police didn't feel the same. Dave had been Acting Detective Superintendent during the murder investigation and, after securing the convictions of Rhys's killer and his cronies, he was expected to be permanently promoted to that role. But, just days after the sentencing finished, Assistant Chief Constable Pat Gallan told him that wasn't going to happen and that he was being returned to his role as to Detective Chief Constable.

Having completed his thirty years' service, Dave was eligible to retire but had been planning to stay on and head up two more murder investigations. After this decision, however, he decided to quit.

When we found out what had happened I was just disgusted and absolutely fuming. I couldn't see any reason why they couldn't give him the promotion. He deserved it. He did everything he could do and got eleven people convicted. Yes, they might have wanted him to do it quicker but that's not the way it works. They were pushing him to make an arrest but he wouldn't be pushed because he wanted to get everybody and do it right. Like he said, 'You only have one go at it so it's got to be right.' If he'd done it quicker he could have got less of a result – if he got any convictions at all. In the end, he not only got Mercer but he got every gang member involved, plus Yates' parents and Mercer's mum as well. But, because they refused to recognise what an amazing job he did, the police force lost a really good police officer and that beggars belief.

Dave never talked it over with us, because that's not something he would do, but we were very upset on his behalf.

He's not just a hero to me and Ste. A lot of people in Liverpool feel the same. When Ste went out for a pint with Dave recently, Ste said that many people were coming over to the two of them, and saying, 'Oh my God, you're the police officer that got those guys.' Everyone was patting him on the back and buying them drinks. Ste said it was just amazing.

Dave said he's never had that before but Ste said, 'It's because you're sitting with me.' People who might not recognise them individually look at them together and click, maybe because they recognise Ste from the papers.

Ste and I try not to think about Mercer and his mates but every now and then something crops up that brings it all flooding back.

As well as Christmas and Rhys's birthday, Mother's Day, as you can imagine, is always a tough day for me.

Although Owen always makes a fuss of me, buying cards and gifts, it's one of those days where I feel the absence of Rhys all the more sharply. But in 2015, the day before Mother's Day, we got a letter to say that James Yates had applied to have an exclusion zone lifted so he could visit Croxteth. He had been released from prison early, in 2014, after serving five years but his parole conditions meant he wasn't allowed anywhere near the area. As a family member was sick, he had asked for this to be temporarily lifted.

Reading the letter made me sick to the bottom of my stomach. I could barely find the words to describe how angry I was. Getting the letter was terrible enough, but to get it twenty-four hours before such an emotional occasion was awful.

Both Ste and I were livid, but it wasn't the first time we'd had to deal with these requests. Coy had asked for something similar when his mum was ill and it had been granted, and a few others have come up as well. We submit our opinions to the parole board but, even though Yates was turned down on that occasion, I'm not sure it matters what we say. If they are going to grant them access to come on to the estate, or to go and see their mums, our opinion doesn't matter.

It is emotionally draining to keep having to deal with these things.

The parole board also called us whenever anyone involved was released, but not until after the event and with very little info about where they are. They won't say, 'Yates is coming out of Walton prison tomorrow.' It would be more like 'Yates has been released,' and that's it. Sometimes it's on the same day and sometimes it's days later. Then we don't know where they are or whether they could come back to Croxteth. Part of the parole is that they don't have any contact and they are not seen in the vicinity but that only lasts for the length of their term and, other than Yates, they have all completed them. The fact that Yates only served five years, after the appeal raised his sentence to twelve years, makes me furious. What was the point?

The papers often drag up reports about what Mercer is doing in prison as well. Some reports claimed he had written to us to say sorry, but he hasn't. We've never had any sign of remorse or regret from him. He probably won't contact us until he's due for parole but anyway, nothing he could say could make me forgive and forget. I'll never forgive him for what he's done or forget the lovely boy he took away from us.

I always read the reports but, to be honest, they just annoy me. They always go on about the cushy life he's having, that he's got an Xbox in his cell and a Liverpool duvet. But he's still in prison, isn't he? So what if he's got this and that and he goes to the gym every day, he's still in prison. That's the only way I can look at it. I can't be looking at it and thinking he's having a good time because, at the end of the day, he is in prison and he doesn't want to be in prison, so it's still punishment, as far as I am concerned.

After his Masters, Owen moved back home for a while, which was good for me. Although I had seen a lot of him while he lived down the road, and he often popped in for his tea, it was lovely to have him there all the time.

Owen soon got a job in Barclays but it wasn't really using his degree. He and his mates always used to joke that none of them actually used the degrees they got in the job they did. Luckily, after a year, Owen got a job that suited him better, as a computer systems analyst – although I have to confess I have no idea what that entails. Initially, it meant quite a lot of travelling for him, going to Nottingham and Bradford and all sorts of other places on a regular basis, but he was home most nights and it was wonderful to see so much of him. He's since moved into another position in Southport, so doesn't have to travel so much, and is now living in his own flat, but we still see a lot of him and his lovely girlfriend, Amaya.

In 2016, I started to worry about our dog, Lennox. He was eleven, which is a good age for a boxer, and I began to notice some odd behaviour.

'I'm sure he's got Alzheimer's,' I said to Ste.

'Don't be daft,' said Ste. 'He's a dog.'

'The dog has got Alzheimer's, I'm telling you,' I said. 'He goes outside and then he stands and looks at me as if to say, "What have I come out here for?"'

'You're stupid, you are,' Ste teased. But I was sure. Sometimes I would watch him trying to get off the floor and really struggling and he did seem a bit lost, so we took him to the vet for a 'senior MOT'.

'Lennox has got Alzheimer's,' the vet said.

'I told you he had Alzheimer's,' I said to Ste. She also explained he was going blind in one eye and had lots of other age-related problems. 'It's up to you if you take him home,' the vet said.

'Oh yeah, we'll take him home,' I said. 'He seems fine.'

About four weeks later, we took him to the cemetery for the first time and he sat beside Rhys's grave, good as gold. The only odd thing was that he would bark occasionally, for no reason, which was unlike him. We have no idea why he would do that but perhaps dogs sense things that we can't.

Two days after the visit to the grave, in the middle of the night, I heard Lennox whining and whining. Ste was at work and Owen was asleep, so I came downstairs to see if I could calm him down. I didn't know what to do but I remembered the breeder saying if he was in pain give him a drop of Calpol, so that's what I did.

Lennox was lying on the floor in the living room so I lay on the couch stroking him. Then Owen got up and went to work and I was supposed to be working too but when Ste came in at half past seven, I said, 'The dog's not right. He can't even stand up.'

Ste lifted him up and tried to get him to stand on his feet and he just fell over, so we took him to the vet and she said it was time to let him go. So we said our goodbyes and he went to sleep. Then I had to phone Owen at work and tell him, which was awful. He came straight home because he was so upset.

The surprising thing to me was how upset *I* was. I was so devastated I had to take two weeks off work. I mean, who takes two weeks off when their dog dies? I surprised myself because I didn't think I was that attached to him but I sobbed and sobbed. Perhaps it was because of his connection with Rhys and I was remembering the bond the pair of them had, but once I started I was inconsolable.

Throughout the trial and to this day, Dave has always been very protective of us over Rhys, even in regards to him doing an interview or someone wanting to talk to him about the case. He would always call us and say, 'Is it OK if I do this? I don't want to do anything without your say-so.'

One evening Dave phoned and asked Ste, 'Have you been contacted by Kwadjo?'

Ste had no idea what he was talking about, so he said, 'Who's Kwadjo?'

'Kwadjo from the telly,' Dave replied.

'I don't know anything, Dave,' said Ste.

'They want to do a film on Rhys,' he said.

'Well, no one's contacted us,' replied Ste.

Dave said he had been talking to the producer, Kwadjo Dajan, about an ITV drama but he was adamant that he wasn't going to agree to anything unless we were on board.

'No one's spoken to us, Dave,' Ste said. 'So I can't say whether we are or we aren't.'

It was a long while before Kwadjo got in touch, as I think the drama was put on the back burner for a while so, to be honest, we had put it to the backs of our minds. But when he called, Ste agreed to meet him. He came round to the house with Dave's former police colleagues Mark McGuinness and Martin Leahy to sound out how we felt about doing it. We weren't sure exactly what they were proposing or whether we would agree to it, but we were prepared to hear them out. For that initial meeting, however, I was at work but I was happy to leave it to Ste to deal with.

Kwadjo came across as a placid, softly-spoken man who seemed honest and genuine about his intentions, and Ste liked him immediately. He told Ste the production company wanted to tell the true story of Rhys's murder, the investigation and the trial, but that they wouldn't do it without our cooperation.

'Look, Kwadjo,' Ste told him. 'There are a couple of things you need to understand. Firstly, it needs to be as accurate as it can be. I don't want you putting in scenes where people are throwing things at the wall or fighting with each other, none of that drama stuff, because that's not us. We are not dramatic people, and we don't throw ourselves on floors and we didn't go out as vigilantes to try to hunt them down.

'Secondly, it has to be a true reflection of Liverpool. Mercer and his gang are not a true reflection of the people who live here. They are a really small minority of the kind that blights most major cities. Most people here are decent.'

We were worried the city would be shown in a bad light but the writer, Jeff Pope, definitely understood that. He later summed it up when he said 'If you think about Mercer as being the bad people of Liverpool, then you think about the 39,000 Evertonians at Goodison who stood up and clapped for a minute as a tribute to Rhys – that's the good side of Liverpool.'

Although Ste had told him we didn't want them doing anything 'Hollywoodised', by putting in scenes that didn't exist, Kwadjo explained that for artistic purposes they might have to put certain things together in certain scenes.

'If it's fact and it happened, that's fine,' said Ste. 'But I'm not letting you invent things to make it more dramatic.'

But Kwadjo explained that they weren't going to do it without our say-so and he said that the likelihood was that someone somewhere was going to make a programme when the tenth anniversary of Rhys's death came around, in 2017. If we weren't involved, someone else could just pick out bits of the story and throw something together that wasn't accurate.

'You have got complete control,' he would tell us. 'If you say you don't want it to go out, or if you don't like it, then fine, we'll stop.' That was always the option he gave us.

After his chat with Kwadjo, Ste talked it through with me and we agreed that we would cooperate. I wasn't worried that the drama was going to drag it all back into the spotlight because I think, and as Kwadjo had said, with the tenth anniversary, that would have happened anyway.

'Do you think they'll do it properly though Ste?' I asked. 'I don't want them putting in stuff that didn't happen, or making us out to be different than we are.'

'They seem pretty genuine,' Ste said. 'They've promised we can pull the plug on anything we don't like and they said we would have the final say.'

Dealing with people in the world of TV drama was a whole new world for us but Ste seemed reassured so that was good enough for me.

In our first meeting with Jeff Pope, the writer, I echoed Ste's earlier points.

'If we're going to do it, it's going to have to be done exactly as it was for us,' I said. 'If you're going to make it into more of a drama than it was, it's not worth doing it.'

'That's exactly what I want too,' he told us. 'At the end of the day you can't change what's gone on. What's happened has happened and you can't do anything to change it, but you can control how it is portrayed on the TV.'

That chat reassured me and made me relax a bit more about giving ITV our blessing to go ahead.

While he was writing the series, which had now been named *Little Boy Blue*, Jeff came to our home and he'd sit and chat over a cup of tea or a glass of wine. We would both tell him our version of events, from the start and all the way through the trial. Incredibly, he didn't record our chats and he never took any notes. Sometimes he would bring a laptop and say, 'Can I just go over this bit because I think I might have missed a bit out.' But it was incredible that he remembered any of it. When we saw the scripts, the dialogue was pretty word-perfect so he must have a very good memory.

Jeff is a great guy. He's so down-to-earth and easy to talk to and we became quite good friends with him over the course of the drama being made. He was as good as his word when it came to consulting us. He went through every script with us, and let us see every scene that was connected with us, and obviously Dave was consulted on all the scenes that affected him.

As they got closer to filming, Sinead Keenan and Brían O'Byrne, who played me and Ste, wanted to meet us to find out what we were really like so we invited them over to the house. They had a cup of coffee and a chat and they were both really nice but it was a strange meeting, because we did feel like they were watching us to pick up our mannerisms. When I finally saw her on screen, I thought Sinead was brilliant but it was pretty weird watching someone play me. I kept thinking, 'Am I really like that?' It's an odd experience.

Kwadjo gave us an open invitation to visit the set whenever we wanted but I didn't want to see any of it. It was too raw. For the trial scenes, they were filming at Liverpool Crown Court, in the very courtroom where Ste and I had sat for eleven weeks and gone through so much, and I really couldn't face going back in there. It would stir up too many painful memories for me.

In the end Ste and Owen went to watch, and the scene they were filming was the lads in the dock, mucking about and being disrespectful. Afterwards, Kwadjo was a bit worried that it might have upset them, so he came over to see if they were OK, and ask what they thought.

'Look, that's exactly what it was like,' Ste told him. 'I'm just glad you're portraying it as it was, so everyone can see what animals they were.'

Ste and I watched the drama prior to it going out and we were both pleased with the way it had been done. It was like a testament to Rhys, which was what we wanted, and it was a true reflection on events, but it was a very hard watch for me. The scenes when Rhys was shot, and the funeral, were too much so we swerved them completely.

The DVD that we watched wasn't the finished cut, so I would imagine that the one that went out on ITV was slightly different but I couldn't bring myself to watch it again. Ste has watched it several times but I have only seen it the once and I won't be watching it again. It's far too traumatic to revisit those memories.

After the series went out, in May 2017, we were inundated with messages. A lot of people were amazed by how both the lads and their parents had behaved.

Because it was such a long trial, people hadn't necessarily taken in all the details that had been reported. Things like their awful behaviour in the dock didn't register in the grand scheme of things, and wasn't often included in the newspaper reports. But when they saw the drama, people were saying, 'Oh my God, is that what happened?'

Some of the things that went on during the trial had been horrific. People told us that when they watched the drama and heard the conversations between Yates's mum and dad, they thought, 'Is this for real? Has somebody made this up?' but it was in the court recording, word for word. It is shocking when you know they are talking about the murder of a little boy, not lads who have been done for shoplifting in the corner shop. A lot of people have said to us, 'How could these people talk like that?' Everyone was shocked by the role the adults played and by how callous and cold and nasty the perpetrators were. Listening to everyone talking about it did bring back some horrible memories of their disgusting attitude in court but I'm glad people now know what they were like.

*Little Boy Blue* was highly praised and was nominated for Best Drama in the TV Choice Awards 2017 and we were invited to attend. So in September, Ste and

I travelled down to London with Dave and Donna, and met up with Jeff Pope and his wife, Tina, before travelling to the Dorchester hotel, where the ceremony was being held.

We were directed to a side entrance into the ballroom, and outside it was all cordoned off, with a red carpet down the centre and photographers and members of the public standing around taking pictures. Jeff had told us it was a black tie event, so Ste and Dave had gone out and bought new shirts and black ties and when we got there, everyone else was dressed in their scruff. Keith Lemon looked like he'd gone to Oxfam for his outfit, Rylan's suit didn't fit him and Katie Price could barely get into hers. It wasn't quite as smart as we'd been led to believe!

There were a whole host of celebrities there, including David Tennant, Phillip Schofield and Holly Willoughby, Paul O'Grady and lots of actors from *Coronation Street*, including Kym Marsh, Catherine Tyldesley, Sam Robertson, who plays Adam Barlow, and Tristan Gemmill, who plays Robert Preston. I have to admit we were all a bit starstruck. It's not every day of the week you're in a room with so many famous faces.

On our table we had Sinead Keenan, who played me in the drama, and Faye McKeever, who played Boy M's mum, then there was Kwadjo and his wife, the director, Paul Whittington, Jeff and his wife and Dave and Donna.

A few of the *Corrie* actors, including Kym Marsh, came over and told us they thought the series was really good and Kym said, 'Great to see you.' Judge Rinder invited me to go and see him in something or other but I'm still waiting for the official invite!

It was a fun night. Jeff explained it wasn't a night when everyone is formal and stuffy. Because it's not that high-profile, and there are no TV cameras inside, everyone gets lashed and has a great time. Quite a few of the celebrities were absolutely leathered.

The wine on the table flowed freely and afterwards Jeff said, 'We are invited to the after-party.' It was in the same place, but they opened a side door that led into a bar area. Jeff went to the bar and got a couple of rounds in and then Dave said, 'Let's go to the bar and get some drinks.' Ste stepped in, as he always does, and said, 'I'll get them.' Big mistake. He got four gin and tonics and a bottle of lager and it was £71! He nearly fell over with shock. It was extortionate.

After we'd finished that drink, Ste said to Dave, 'It's your round mate.'

Dave came back with, 'We're getting off now,' so he dodged that one – but not without a good ribbing from Ste!

We were staying in the same hotel as Faye, in Marble Arch. She got in the first taxi in the line and we got in a second, but our driver somehow managed to get lost. When we eventually got back to our hotel, Faye had persuaded the manager to open the bar up, so we had a few more drinks in there. It was a great night.

The drama did bring Rhys's murder back to the forefront of the nation's mind but in Liverpool, to be honest, it has never gone away.

I still can't go anywhere without being recognised. If Ste and I go out in the city centre, we will be approached at least four times in a night. I don't mind when people say, 'Hiya, are you OK?' or pat us on the back – it's when they pull up a chair and sit down with us like we're old friends it gets a bit too much.

On the whole, though, people are respectful and sympathetic. As I said before, there are some bad eggs out there but 99 per cent of Liverpudlians are decent, considerate, good people.

The tenth anniversary of Rhys's death, on 22 August 2017, was a huge day for us. We wanted to mark the date and do something special to remember Rhys by, so we put a new headstone on his grave, inscribed with the poem that Ste had written for his funeral.

That poem, with lines like 'Glistening eyes and cheeky face, angel's halo out of place ...' summed him up so perfectly and it moves me to tears every time I read it.

On the day, we visited the grave and laid fresh flowers, as we always do on the anniversary. We spent all day there chatting to him about all sorts, and various friends and family came by with flowers, including Rhys's childhood friends, all grown up now and either in university or in work. It breaks my heart looking at them and wondering what Rhys would have been doing now, thinking of all that young potential he was robbed of in a split second.

My visits to the grave are among the many routines that keep me going, and able to cope. I still light the candles for him every night, without fail, and kiss his picture goodnight before I go to bed, and I visit Rhys at least twice a week, by myself in the week and with

Ste at the weekend. I have to do that, and I begin to get anxious if I don't.

At least once a week we take fresh flowers – always yellow and white roses, mainly because we don't like red ones and Rhys wouldn't have liked anything red anyway. If we go to the florist and they don't have the right flowers, it's a disaster. I get into a proper panic. It's not too bad around August because there are no big dates, like Valentine's Day or Mother's Day, so they are usually fairly available.

The grave is pretty simple and uncluttered, and the roses fit in perfectly. Plus, because we spend a decent amount on them, they last really well, as long as it's not roasting hot. If the last ones are still good we might take them out and put them in a pot by the side, then put the fresh ones on the grave.

While I'm there I talk to Rhys about everything. I tell him about the game, I told him when Rooney came back to Everton, which he would have loved. I give him updates about what's going on and tell him, 'Owen's coming for his tea with his girlfriend. You would have liked her.' Everyday stuff.

Apart from the gravestone, we didn't mark the tenth anniversary any differently from the way we have marked them in previous years but for me personally, it was a big deal. I didn't think I'd ever get to his tenth anniversary. I didn't think I would be able to make it this far. Then suddenly it's ten years and you can't believe that a whole decade has passed. It's such a long time and yet, to us, it often feels like yesterday.

I still miss everything about him, every day. I miss his laugh, his voice, his smile. I miss his muddy football boots and filthy football kit. I miss him charging about the house and wrestling the dog. I miss him giving me a hug. Before I lost Rhys I wouldn't have thought it was physically possible to cry as many tears as I have cried in the last ten years.

Ste, Owen and I are getting on with our lives and have somehow learned to live with the huge void left by Rhys and carry on. There's no alternative and nothing will bring him back. But as long as we live we will never forget our Little Boy Blue.

# EPILOGUE

God Wanted a Football Match
**by Stephen Jones**

Now God wanted a football match
And to play it up in heaven
But first he needed players
And select his first eleven

Georgie Best, big Brian Labone
The legend Dixie Dean
Alan Ball and Bobby Moore
All made it in the team

He needed one more player
Someone who would be quick
From up above he looked down
And saw Rhys there in his kit

So Rhys was taken up above
God took him by the hand
To play the game he loved so much
Where sponsorship is banned

There is no cheating either as
God is the referee
There are no mega wages
And the transfers they are free

The games are live on telly
You don't have to subscribe
The players all stay on their feet
Cos no one takes a dive

So Rhys plays now so happily
To the angels in the crowd
And every time he hits the net
They roar his name so loud

Have fun my little blue boy
You're safe and in God's care
Till it's time for me to get my boots
And join with you up there

# ACKNOWLEDGEMENTS

I would like to thank my husband Ste, who has been a tower of strength through our darkest times, and all our wonderful family and friends for their support and love. For their hard work and determination I will be forever grateful to Dave Kelly and his team at Merseyside Police. I would also like to thank the Reverend Harry Ross, Everton Football Club, Liverpool Football Club, the City of Liverpool and Tesco for their help and support. Finally, thank you to Alison Maloney for helping me to put Rhys's story onto the page.